Acknowled

I am very grateful to Margaret Taylor .... in designing and executing the cover of this book.

On seeing the cover, as the book was being prepared for the Press, an unkind critic commented:

'There is no need to read this book. The cover alone is sufficient indication of its contents, and also reveals much about the author. Here is to be seen a character definitely at sea, with a lot of wind, but no direction, with delusions of musical grandeur, blowing his own trumpet and getting his (fishy) friends to do all the work.'

The reader must form his own opinion on the justice of these comments; but I trust that he will enjoy the cover nonetheless as much as I have done.

B.W.R.

An Amateur in Music

B. W. Robinson

COUNTRYSIDE BOOKS
NEWBURY, BERKSHIRE

First published 1985
© B. W. Robinson

COUNTRYSIDE BOOKS
3 Catherine Road
Newbury, Berkshire

ISBN 0 905392-52-3

Produced through MRM (Print Consultants) Ltd, Reading
Typeset in England by Acorn Bookwork, Salisbury, Wilts
Printed by Penwell Ltd, Parkwood, Callington, Cornwall

Contents

Preface

There are surprisingly few books addressed to the amateur in music. Yet the amateur, in the broadest sense of the term, is the mainstay of music, the vehicle of its existence, historically and financially the medium in which it develops. Why then is there no mention of him as such in the average encyclopaedia; why is there no 'Oxford Companion to Amateur Music', perhaps as a supplement to Scholes' masterpiece?

A general survey of Amateur Music would be a fascinating task. But even if I had the knowledge and energy to attempt it, I should not live long enough to complete it. The present work started as a few factual descriptions of music I had enjoyed – as performer, not as listener – omitting large areas of amateur music (brass bands, amateur opera, 'popular' music for example, about which I know nothing). Friendly critics considered these to be indigestible as they stood – 'dry bread, with no butter or jam' was the phrase used – and I was urged to abandon the original anonymity and to say much more about the Music Camp, with which I had been chiefly associated in the music I had done. Then I found that there were several comments I wanted to make on practical amateur music; my friends went for musical holidays, their children flocked to youth orchestras and choirs, they played chamber music, some of them were concerned with finance in arranging for concerts; all these topics seemed worthy of mention. So, in various directions, the book, like Topsy, 'just growed'. It is full of omissions; it is not a book of instruction (though it generalizes about conducting and rehearsing); nor is it a work of reference (though it contains an amateur's bibliography); but I hope that it reflects something of the activities and interests of a group of friends who have found in playing and singing music an abiding pleasure and excitement for much of their lives. Besides the theme of friendship, another question links parts of the book together – the difficult one 'why do we do music as amateur performers anyway?'

The debt to my friends is obvious throughout, and I will not attempt to thank them individually. But of course I take full responsibility for any mistakes of fact, or for opinions which further enquiry would perhaps have modified.

I make no apology for the fact that I have no professional qualifications in music, and I claim no special musical ability or technical knowledge beyond that of a good amateur. But I am proud to be an amateur musician; and if this book can interest other amateurs and help them at all to increase their pleasure in music – perhaps even to encourage some professionals occasionally to enjoy music more like amateurs – then it will have served a useful purpose.

1
Introduction: The Amateur

One point I must make clear from the start – the meaning of this word, which will recur frequently in this book.

In modern speech, 'amateur' is sometimes associated with the slipshod, the casual, the unskilled, etc – an association which I wish to repudiate. For the purposes of this book, 'amateur' means exclusively what its etymology suggests – 'one who loves music', but who does not depend on it as the main source of his income. Of course there are many amateurs who are unskilled; some have no natural facility in the execution of music; some are self-taught and may have had little time to spend on their chief pleasure; few will have tackled the kind of discipline which is necessary even to approach a good professional technique. But no-one who has watched the faces of a good chorus singing the Mass in B minor, or observed the labours by which some double-bass player – possibly a very poor performer – transports his instrument to the weekly rehearsal, will admit the words 'slipshod' or 'casual'. The amateur is a lover, maybe an inexperienced and clumsy one, but not a disillusioned husband.

Part of the impetus to attempt this book came in fact from an unfortunate use of this word, in the columns of the *Radio Times*, where a University Professor of Music, writing about the broadcast of his new opera, lamented the 'amateur' atmosphere in which his work was normally carried on. But is it not the business of such a one to be ready to work with amateurs, and to judge his success, at least in part, by the number of students who leave his University, not as trained musicians, but as amateurs with an enhanced love for and experience of music?

I think that many amateurs too easily accept their lowly position in the eyes of many laymen, and indeed of some professionals. A visitor from Mars, wishing to find out what music on this Earth was all about, and introduced to some big dictionary, would get a very wrong impression. He would find plenty about composers, history, composition, technique and musicology of all sorts; but unless his reading was carefully guided it would be a long time before he had much evidence that the musical amateur existed today, or was of importance in music at all.

And yet, in the body musical, the amateur is the flesh and blood. Without him, the skilled hands and trained ears of the executant, and the brain and imagination of the composer, would waste away. So is he not worth some small fraction, one per cent perhaps, of the text of 'Grove'? I am sure that Sir George himself would not have countenanced such neglect – he who addressed his classic work on the Beethoven Symphonies 'to the amateurs of this country'; it was 'his humble endeavour to convey to others the method by which an amateur has obtained much pleasure and profit out of works which in their own line are as great as Shakespeare's plays.'

Amateur music making and listening may in fact be likened to a vast iceberg which supports the glamorous and expensive professional tip. I think that the amateur needs reminding of the size and variety of the business interests concerned, for which he is the chief consumer and paymaster. We can do no better than to study the pages of the *British Music Yearbook* (ref 1) (if we have never done so before), and make some estimate of the amount of the money which comes from our pockets.

Most of us contribute as taxpayers to the half million pounds annually distributed by the Arts Council to music; similarly, as ratepayers, to the rates allocated by most local Councils to music, and as licence holders to the BBC's income, more than £700 million p.a., much of which goes to the music industry. Additionally, as purchasers of records, tapes, musical instruments and electronic equipment we support an army of publishers, manufacturers and retailers – 200 record companies, 140 manufacturers and, say, 1,000 retailers are listed in the Yearbook, and each presumably has an annual turnover from the tens of thousands to the millions (about 450 million gramophone records were sold in this country in 1982, of which perhaps 10% might be of 'serious' music).

The tale is not complete. On the more individual side of expenditure, as pupils, we support at least 2,400 private teachers (shall we say at a minimum of £5,000 p.a.); then, as subscribers to concert clubs, choral and orchestral societies (of which some 1,100, with a combined membership, say, of 100,000, are listed in the handbook of the National Federation of Music Societies (ref. 2), we pay at least £20 per year, or £2M in all; and finally, as concert-goers, we buy tickets; I have not tried to find out how much in all, but obviously the total receipts from the Festival Hall and Albert Hall and Covent Garden alone must be a very large sum.

This is a very crude list of the ways in which the amateur spends money on music; however inaccurate my estimates may be, the total is immense, and this money eventually goes into the pockets of the professional musician in part, but even more I imagine into those of the commercial and administrative gentlemen who gather round him. It is interesting to speculate on what would be the national reaction to an amateurs' strike, of players, singers and listeners – no concert audiences, no record sales or music lessons for a year perhaps; we could all go home and practice, maybe to our eventual benefit.

The vast growth of this multi-million pound industry over the past 30 years is of course largely due to modern electronics, with its encouragement of the passive listener. But fortunately many of us find that our hi-fi and our TV is not enough – given the opportunity and the incentive, we can be practical musicians, we can dance, stamp, play and sing in active involvement. And we find that our pleasure is of a different kind from what we may enjoy just as listeners.

In no other art, except perhaps the amateur drama, is the amateur performer so much needed. However useful he may have been in the last century, maybe as botanist or astronomer, today the amateur scientist can make little contribution to knowledge; as amateur artist, he is unlikely to paint a picture of permanent value; as amateur architect, he will never have a chance to design a cathedral. But in music the amateur is needed all the time. In the privacy of his home he may sometimes think with justification, 'I have re-created this sound as well as Haydn (or perhaps even Beethoven) ever heard it'; and together with his fellows he may join in a good choral performance and know that he is an essential part of this great structure of sound. Music has to be performed; it would not survive for long if its practice were confined to score-reading and music-ology.

And how varied are the ways in which I, as an amateur, can enjoy myself, as compared with my professional brother! Free from doubts as to whether it is financially worth my while, or whether my reputation is in the balance, I can choose that aspect of music which I enjoy most. As a hi-fi expert, proud of my latest equipment, I can contrast A's performance with B's; as a keen singer or player, even at a lowly level, I can enjoy the pleasures of steady hard work and progress and of cooperating with my fellows; I may travel with a cheerful party to a brass band performance, or throw away inhibitions and cheer with the rest at the last night of the 'Proms'; I may entertain three old friends to supper, to be followed by yet another attack on a Bartók quartet, topped off by a gay Haydn. Of all arts, music is the most social; man turns to music when he is sad or when he is happy; Pan, Orpheus and Bacchus alike must have their music. Those who claim superior sensibility may scoff at the weekly rehearsal or at the monthly concert club as more a social than a musical occasion; nevertheless, I feel that it is better than Bingo (without attempting to draw any moral, I might interpolate that the one-time controller of Bingo for a very large organization has always sought his pleasure, not in gambling, but as a first-class amateur oboist).

I have already said that this book is for the performer, rather than the listener. There are superior people who maintain that amateurs should not perform for other people to listen (does this perhaps mean that they never listen to big choral concerts?). It is true that some amateur performances are only tolerable when heard in their proper context of effort and enthusiasm. But nowadays one can hear many others which are worth listening to without any qualification. Sometimes even difficult 20th century works are tackled in a manner not to be despised, technically good enough to give a very good idea of what the music is all about. The main reason for an amateur performance may well be the pleasure of the performers; but this pleasure may spread to the listeners too.

My own pleasure in music has certainly been on the active rather than the passive side, and I believe that the deepest feelings in music are more likely to be reached when one has attempted, however imperfectly, to express them oneself in playing and singing. Eric Blom for example says (ref. 10) 'There is no short cut to the mystery of an inspired work of art by way of another person's effort. To know Beethoven's op. 106 (the 'Hammerklavier') we must, as Sir Toby would say, accost it, front it, board it, woo it, assail it. And we must do it at the piano, however badly the music may fare at our hands'.

And even the bad amateur performer may take heart from Vaughan Williams, who says (ref. 4), 'My next sermon is addressed not to the professional musician but to the amateur, and especially to the listener, and my text is "Be ye doers of the Word, not hearers only". A musical nation is not a nation which is content to listen. The best form of musical appreciation is to try and do it for yourself; to get really inside the meaning of music. If I were to visit a strange country and wanted to find out if it had a real musical life, I should not go to the great cities with their expert orchestras, their opera houses and their much advertised celebrity concerts, but I should go to the small towns and villages and find out there whether enthusiastic quartet parties met once a week, whether there was a madrigal club, whether music was a normal form of recreation in their homes, whether the people met to sing or play together under their local leader, whether they encouraged that leader to create music for the pageants and ceremonies of their town, whether they saw to it that the music in their churches was worthy of the liturgies performed there.'

2
Music Camp and its Relations

Early Experiences

I was brought up, from a musical point of view, in a limited way; my father had no knowledge of music, my mother sang in the church choir with an occasional solo; we had no general musical education, no piano, no gramophone or radio while we were children. The first musical experience I can remember was at the age of 6, hearing the 'Messiah' performed by a village choir in Yorkshire. At 9, I was singing in the church choir, knew 'Messiah' well, and could (I think) read a simple choral line. My sisters and I had violin lessons of an elementary kind with the village newsagent – a nice old boy, but even by my childish standards it did not seem that he could play the fiddle very well. The first (and, in relation to income, the largest) professional fee that I ever received was at the age of 12, being half a crown for playing hymns at one of the 'Pleasant Sunday Afternoons' of the period. (Archie Camden was better paid: he got 5/- for his first professional fee at the age of 9 – but he was probably much more than twice as good as I was).

Saying good-bye to the music teacher at my first school (I was not a pupil of his, but I had been listening to his playing of a Beethoven sonata), I remember his saying 'Young Robinson, if you go on with music when you are older, you can take it from me – you will find that musical women are the devil.' In retrospect, I have often wondered what drama must have been the background to this unsolicited remark to a lad of 13. I am very glad that it did not prevent me from marrying two very distinguished 'musical women' later in life!

At my next school, Oundle, there was a fair amount of music, though not at all as much as there would be nowadays at a school of such reputation. I met such works as the 'Unfinished' and Mozart in G minor in the rather incomplete school orchestra (for some time the only brass player of any kind was a cornet player). Surprisingly, at some point in this period I got to know the notes of Beethoven's 'Emperor' piano concerto – the solo had been practised by a school friend, and we joined in the holidays with my sisters with the orchestral part 'rendered' from music copied by myself from the piano arrangement – I doubt that I ever saw a full score. But it was a great thrill, later at the age of 16, to go to my first 'Prom' and hear this work properly played – Leonard Borwick was the soloist – and to realize for the first time what a good orchestra sounded like. This work has ever since been my favourite of all concertos.

At Cambridge from 1922 till 1927, though officially reading Physics, I covered a good deal of musical ground, and for the first time played in chamber music with good teams. I met Alan Richards – usually considered to be the best amateur violinist around; he became a lifelong friend. Alan was also a passable flautist, and a pleasant baritone singer; he was particularly good at the 'Et in Spiritum Sanctum' from the B minor Mass. He was the only amateur member of a distinguished string-playing family.

A major occasion to me was a quartet to which I was summoned (together with Alan) to play with Bessie Rawlins and her husband Frank Winton, who were staying near Cambridge for a few weeks. This was the first time I had ever met a really first-class player, who knew all the music and had only one standard – the best. She disguised the kindest of hearts under her habit of the uncompromising statement of truth, as she saw it, and was frightening but also tremendously inspiring to an amateur like myself, who was facile but had no basic technique. The progression from 'Why don't you learn a little about how to play your instrument?' soon after I first met her, to 'Well, really, you played that quite well' (a Mozart viola part), forty years later, was indeed a rewarding one and summarised, I suppose, several thousands of hours playing under her leadership, mainly with Frank and Alan.

At Christmas 1925 a plan was formed to learn more about the B minor Mass, originally with a vocal quintet and a string quartet round the piano. (I have since been told that this was an unconscious echo of a more distinguished party which had gathered for a similar purpose (the 'St Matthew Passion'), in Mendelssohn's house about 100 years earlier). The party swelled quickly into a tiny chorus and orchestra (with compromises; I remember that clarinets played alternately oboi d'amore and trumpets), perhaps 50 people in all, in the dining-room of Regents Park College in London, to which my father had recently come as Principal. This was a play-through, without rehearsal. We repeated it next year, with larger numbers and were joined by one or two professionals, who volunteered their help in a most generous manner. Margaret Balfour was one, resplendent in a concert dress for the Queen's Hall, where she was singing that evening; and Ursula Nettleship joined the party, a lady who had a great effect on my life, among other things in introducing me to my first wife, Alice. Ursula sang the 'Laudamus' in a way which has spoilt me for anyone else since then, by heart, and with her beautiful face radiating happiness.

Music Camp had not started by then (1925 and 1926), but this gathering was in effect the beginning of the 'Music Camp Reunions' which have continued at the New Year as an unbroken series since then; at first, always the B minor Mass; later, in rotation with one or two other big works fitted to the occasion.

Beginnings of Music Camp

At Cambridge I had tried my hand with a little conducting, and made many musical friendships, as with the Beavans, Butterworths, Richards, McCormick families, and with Boris Ord, always an inspiration to amateurs. So in 1927 several of us decided to try a musical holiday together. We were mostly impecunious students, and camping was the cheapest way to live; we found a small village hall in Poynders End, in Hertfordshire, with a nearby field to camp in. With a few borrowed tents and some elementary kitchen gear the first Music Camp, 35-strong, assembled in 1927 (the name was not at first liked, but it has persisted). The experiment was successful and was repeated.

The next important date was 1930, when, having met Edric Cundell at a chamber music party in London, I persuaded him to join us. It was remarkable that this distinguished musician enjoyed himself so much at Music Camp, at a period when the average standard musically was low, compared with what it became a few years later. But his personal qualities and his abounding love of music – which to him was not a means of livelihood or a means of display, but simply and sufficiently a way of life – together with his later connections as Principal of the Guildhall School of Music, had a great effect on the general standard and reputation of Music Camp. We were indeed fortunate in finding him, and also in the friendliness and interest of several other distinguished musicians over the period 1930–39, who came to Music Camp first perhaps out of curiosity – for it was a new departure in amateur music – and found to their surprise that they wanted to come again. Steuart Wilson, I believe, was asked by someone how he could enjoy such a group of amateurs; he replied 'I know of no other group who would let me conduct a Beethoven symphony.' To have Bessie Rawlins and her husband Frank (in those days one of the best amateur 'cellists around) always ready to play late Beethoven quartets to us in the evenings, and several good players from the Boyd Neel Orchestra, Bernard Brown, Leonard and Dennis Brain one year, Archie Camden conducting and playing timpani – altogether it was an exciting party, both personally and musically, in the days when the standard of amateur music as a whole was a long way below that of the bright young people of today. Great was the exhilaration of getting to know the major works of music together, by the best of all methods, that of trying them out; fifty years later, it is hard to remember how little we knew of what is nowadays almost taken for granted by the musical teenager.

For the earliest years the Camps were held in a variety of sites; some were not very suitable, and a kitchen, for example, might have to be improvised literally from a cowshed. A great advance was in 1935, when an old friend of my wife, Gerald Palmer, agreed to find room for us on his estate near Newbury in Berkshire and to give us a long lease of a site (Bothampstead) which became the home of the Music Camp for the next thirty years. Here there was an old Malthouse and Barn attached, with a field; there was water (but no electricity) available, the building was solid and reasonably spacious, and there was very pleasant country around, close to the Berkshire Downs. Here a regular routine could be established; things did not have to be reconstructed each time entirely from zero, and we could begin to acquire and store our own property, such as chairs, tables, tents, and kitchen equipment.

There were now regularly two Camps, each of nine days, each summer; and the general principles were established which have persisted ever since, and have been largely responsible for the success of the Camps, viz: no passengers (everyone must justify his place by what he can contribute, as musician, cook, or handyman); all labours are shared (everyone takes a turn at the chores); and no absentees (everyone must be there all the time). Such principles were never exactly formulated as a dogma or code, but they grew up naturally among a body of people who knew each other very well, and most of whom had competence at one thing or another.

Comfort at those early Camps was (by present standards) rather Spartan; but we were almost all young people, much of an age, and in fact enjoying the hard work involved in setting up and taking down each Camp; the labours of handling tents, filling palliasses, digging latrines and producing tolerable food with Primus stoves and a few utensils, were worthwhile. We managed very cheaply and had no financial resources; remarkable expedients were adopted to save money, such as a lighting system built from an old car engine and a second-hand dynamo, anxiously watched by our chief engineer during rehearsals. Our first generous present was of 60 chairs from Miss Olive Willis, headmistress of the nearby Downe House School. It was a great help when mains electricity came to Bothampstead, and the kitchen department began to acquire reasonable equipment.

The War of course caused a considerable alteration; full Camps were discontinued from 1941 to 1945, starting again in 1946. Two or three weekends were, however, held each summer during this period, for anyone who was able to turn up, and could furnish himself with a few 'points' and coupons to help in feeding arrangements. A surprising number of people managed to turn up for these impromptu music parties, and to form a workable team; I can remember a Haydn symphony where for a time the only bass instrument was a tuba! A series of similar parties was also held in London for a time every couple of months, at the Guildhall School of Music.

One accident – nothing to do with enemy action – was in the winter of 1941, when a fire destroyed the contents of the Malthouse, including furniture, instruments and music, which ironically had been stored there for safety from the bombs of London. What seemed at first to be a disaster proved eventually to be to our benefit; for it made us realize that a group of young people, including many who had technical experience of all sorts, could in fact undertake a good deal of amateur building as well as music. The landlord was sympathetic and allowed us to do anything within reason; and from 1946 energetic 'working parties' cleared the ruined site, re-roofed the Malthouse, and eventually widened the original Barn. The result was a set of buildings much better for our purposes than the originals of 1935; a dining room that could seat 100, a Barn rather narrow but quite possible for chorus and orchestra together, and an extension in

which the chorus could rehearse separately. The 'Phoenix', model-
led somewhat robustly in concrete, which we placed proudly on the
apex of the roof, still stands there today.

Music Camp continued to expand, slightly in numbers (limited by
the space available in rehearsal and dining room, but also by the
feeling that 100–120 was as large as a party of this kind should be);
and notably in musical scope and standard. I will continue, later in
this Chapter, with its development after about 1946; meanwhile I
will mention my own involvement in some other directions.

Other Activities

In 1933 I became the conductor of the Royal Amateur Orchestral
Society. This orchestra was one of the oldest amateur bodies in this
country; it was founded in the 1870s at the instance of the then Duke
of Edinburgh and gave its first concert in the Albert Hall; Arthur
Sullivan was its first conductor. For a long time it was a wealthy and
fashionable orchestra, engaging distinguished soloists of the day,
giving frequent concerts patronized by Royalty, founding scholar-
ships and giving money for charitable purposes. In 1933 however it
had considerably declined from this position. It had largely lost its
contact with youth and did not recruit the new generation of better
amateurs, for whom there were available more attractive orchestras,
of higher standard. Many old players had been in their seats it
seemed for generations – it may be imagination, but I seem to
remember one aged viola player who tapped me on the shoulder and
said 'Young man, Sir Arthur Sullivan didn't take it as fast as that.'
And one of the first things I had to do as conductor was to tell the
Committee that I could not possibly continue rehearsals without a
replacement for the first oboe (a member of the committee).

An interesting episode with this orchestra resulted from the
announcement that H.M. King George was prepared to attend a
concert. So a grand programme was set up for a charity concert in
the Albert Hall in May 1934. Three distinguished soloists – Tauber,
Eva Turner and Conchita Supervia – were engaged, the orchestra
was greatly augmented by all the good amateurs and young students
that I and others could collect, totalling eventually some 90 players;
Sir Henry Wood agreed to conduct, and I had the pleasure of playing
'Fantasia on British Sea Songs' on the timpani to close this pro-

gramme under his baton. It was indeed a lesson in efficiency to watch his handling of this heterogenous assortment of players.

But the orchestra as a whole was unwilling, it seemed to me, to change its ways and to do the necessary hard work to produce a real improvement (it should be said that after various difficulties and vicissitudes and changes of conductor it survived the War, and eventually settled down to a pleasant and stable existence under its present conductor, Arthur Davison). So I resigned in 1936, and set up a small orchestra of my own on very different lines, the Informal Chamber Orchestra. This was a group of about 20 strings, with single or double woodwind and horns as needed, and trumpets, timpani, etc. occasionally. I aimed at including only players with whom I could enjoy playing chamber music; Alan Richards was the leader, Eric Halfpenny double bass, and Handel Knott first horn – names well known in amateur music at the time. Fritz Spiegl, Hubert Brand, Victor Robinson, Robin Lock, Gavin Park, and Geoffrey Hartley were for considerable periods leading players in our woodwind. We worked hard at the smaller symphonies and other suitable works, and, I think, gave very good performances, perhaps three or four times a year, mainly to schools (Harrow, Charterhouse, Haileybury, Rugby, for example), or to invited audiences of our friends. Many rising young soloists appeared with us in concertos. Our expenses were mainly for rehearsal rooms and were covered by subscription and the small sums (say £15 in those early days, plus travel and hospitality) paid to us by schools. Later on, we found it advantageous financially (as did many other amateur groups) to get adopted as an official 'evening class' by the ILEA; this provided a rehearsal room and instructor's fees which could go into the orchestra chest. I remained organizer and conductor of this orchestra with great personal and musical satisfaction, for thirty years.

As performer, rather than conductor, it was an interesting experience to be fitted out in a brown velvet suit and play in the stage band in the Glyndebourne productions of 'Don Giovanni' in 1938 and 1939. In those days, there was quite an amateur touch about Glyndebourne – in the sense that everyone was enjoying themselves under John Christie's genial patronage; the technique and devotion was in the highest degree professional, of course. It was most instructive to see how hard these fine singers worked – Baccaloni as Leporello, Helletsgruber as Elvira I remember in particular. A good time was had by all, and there were many good friends in the orchestra (I suppose that nowadays the Musician's Union would cancel the whole Glyndebourne season rather than have a handful of amateurs in the stage band!). I have since then been able to say, with perfect truth, on the right occasion, that my only operatic performing experience has been on the Glyndebourne stage, and even that, when assembling a souvenir programme, some 25 years later, the editor insisted on including my photograph (a small blob in one corner of the big scene at the end of Act 1 of 'Don Giovanni'!).

In 1936 I also started a group of some 20 singers, the Informal Singers, which worked hard at such unaccompanied pieces as the Debussy and Ravel 'Chansons', with, of course, Renaissance music. We gave occasional private concerts; but the War brought our rehearsals to an end, and they were not started again afterwards, when there were several good small groups of this kind growing up.

At the beginning of the War I moved to the Royal Aircraft Establishment at Farnborough, to work on aircraft instrument design, and met several good musicians who have remained my friends since then. While working there I organized groups of such singers and players as were to hand, for various occasions in the Farnborough–Farnham–Woking area; several 'Messiah's and a B minor Mass, if I remember aright, somewhat under difficulties in wartime conditions. For a time I directed the Aldershot Choral Society. When I had to leave Farnborough, I handed over this Society to a certain Miss Ruth Railton – an unknown name to me at the time, but later to become so well known with the National Youth Orchestra.

A little later on, for a couple of years I conducted the Newbury Amateur Orchestral Society, a society of long standing, probably typical of many of the smaller local orchestras at the time; also I had some responsibility for the undergraduate music at University College, London.

Later Years

I return now to the Music Camp from about 1946, the re-roofing and general clearance after the fire in 1941 having resulted in a considerable improvement in the site from our point of view. The original brickwork inside the Malthouse and the big iron grid on which the malt had been treated were no longer there; we constructed one or two interior rooms for library and storage and removed some party walls to give space for a dining room, rather awkwardly shaped but adequate. In the light of our later experience, our methods were crude and our equipment inadequate. But we learnt a lot and enjoyed ourselves thoroughly.

The general pattern of Music Camp had by this time become very largely what it remains today, its purpose summarized in an early Camp circular as 'the serious rehearsal of the major works of music, by a competent team of friends, close-knit, self-sufficient, and free from other distractions'. With numbers kept to about 120, only a slow change in membership, no publicity, no formal audience, no necessity to rehearse for concerts as such, this purpose was attained. Recruitment was by personal contact only; there were usually not more than 20 newcomers at any Camp, so that the average 'life' at Camp was six or seven years: a few did not fit in and did not return after their first visit, but many continued for much longer times; up to the mid-seventies there were still quite a number of the 'old originals' of 1927–30.

In a normal programme, the mornings were spent in separate chorus and orchestra rehearsal, the evenings in joint rehearsal; the afternoons were not formally planned, but of course a great deal of chamber music, madrigal singing, etc. took place. Two, sometimes three, conductors were kept busy, and occasionally visiting soloists appeared, though they were never a main feature of the music planning; for many works, soloists would be found among the normal Camp membership.

There was a steady improvement in the technical standard of the music and in the range of works attempted. Bothampstead was a beautiful site and had accumulated sentimental memories for most of us. But it was rather constricted, both in music and in camping space; as was felt in a major effort such as that of 1952, when we decided for the first time to stage an opera ('Fidelio'), as described in a later chapter, and had to dig a special pit for the orchestra and go to great trouble to squeeze in stage, scenery, and audience seats. Though we had the sole use of the buildings, it became clear in the early 1960s that we were something of a nuisance to the farm bailiff, whose cottage adjoined our main building; there was also a likelihood that the new construction for the M4 Motorway would pass very close to us. So there were good reasons for looking round for another site.

In 1963 my wife and I found an even better site for the Music Camp, which we managed to buy – Pigotts, an old farmhouse and buildings in the Chilterns, suitably isolated in beechwoods at the top of a steep hill – this time with electricity but no water! It had been the final home of the distinguished artist and stone-carver Eric Gill and was in most respects ideal for our purpose. Though there were two moderate-sized barns, neither was big enough for the full Camp rehearsals; but by 1965 we had managed to get mains water available, and by summoning up our financial resources and building skills – the latter well developed at Bothampstead – we added a building of nearly 3000 sq. ft. area, free from the internal pillars which had been an impediment at Bothampstead, entirely by amateur labour. Our new building has turned out to be excellent, both in convenience and in acoustics.

So in 1965 we made the move – a momentous decision, and for some a sad one, after 30 years of occupancy, during which some complete families had grown up with Bothampstead as their musical background. The occasion was celebrated by a farewell party to 'Lady Bothampstead' – the eccentric but aristocratic Lady of the Manor who had made several previous appearances when occasion demanded. Now in the character of Semele, summoned by Jupiter to join him on Olympus, she received musical and poetic tributes from each department of Camp in turn, and was finally hoisted aloft (to the limits of the roof) to the strains of Handel's final chorus, and an impressive pyrotechnic display.

Since we have settled at Pigotts, the availability of a permanent site, in occupation all the year round, has made, and is still making, a big difference to Music Camp. Though the main building is not suitable or designed for winter use, smaller rooms are reasonably comfortable for most of the year, and it is possible to accommodate groups of 30 to 40 sleeping under cover. Many weekends therefore are nowadays devoted to smaller parties, not necessarily musical ones; there is a strong connection through my headmaster son Nicholas with several schools who use Pigotts e.g. for dramatic rehearsals, revision for examinations, or just social parties. In addition, major musical events have grown in size and frequency much beyond the 'two Camps a year' of the early days, to include many Strauss and Wagner operas in concert version, and all manner of baroque-sized singing and playing groups, experimental music, major chamber music parties, and so forth. A 'Junior Music Camp' for 60 or so young people is usually held over the Whitsun Holiday, and Imperial College Choir arranges a four-day rehearsal as an annual feature. The whole of 'The Ring' is planned for a series of these week-end parties, which is about half-way through at the moment (84–85); this is a large-scale undertaking, with a full and excellent orchestra of up to 100 players, organised by Bob Montgomery and conducted by Nicholas Braithwaite.

It has even become possible to stage a number of operas; a big effort, with the work of building stage, lighting and scenery in these unusual conditions, but an inspiring challenge to the producer. The results have been remarkable; 'Figaro', 'West Side Story', and 'The Rake's Progress' have had their turn, and I realized a long-standing ambition by conducting Bartók's 'Duke Bluebeard's Castle' in an unusual and effective production, in which two dancers paralleled in their dancing the emotions of the singers: I believe a unique solution to the problems of putting this masterpiece on the stage.

The finances of Music Camp are simple enough, since all its enterprises are strictly amateur; there are no fees or 'expenses' paid to anyone, even to the hard-working cooks and conductors. Consequently the main expense of any party is the prime cost of food, with power and heating. The cost of administration is mainly in postage and telephone; the hire of music is a steadily increasing item, but for many works the Elizabeth Library is available; a share in rates for the buildings is also reckoned in the total cost. So for each party the subscription, contributed by everyone who takes part, can be adjusted to cover the cost, with a little over for small building works (which are pretty continuous) and general wear and tear, replacement of utensils, etc. Some of the parties at non-camp times contribute much in the way of skilled and unskilled work in maintenance, gardening, etc. The original subscription to Music Camp in 1927 was £2; now in 1984 it was £39, a figure roughly equivalent in purchasing power to the original one, and only possible because of the unpaid services continually given by so many devoted helpers.

Everyone who comes to Pigotts is treated as, and is expected to behave as, an invited guest; this simple formula solves a multitude of problems, and seems to work very well.

I have already said that a 'Reunion' in London at the New Year has been an unbroken feature of Music Camp from the earliest days; to it all active members of Camp are invited, and a great many come to sing, even if their camping days are over; over a weekend a major work is rehearsed and performed to an audience of friends. A large hall is of course needed for this occasion; for many years we used the hall of Queen Mary College, but for the last couple of years that of the City University. It has been a great privilege in my life to have been able to conduct such an excellent team on these occasions; the B minor Mass has been the favourite work, with some 25 performances; Beethoven's 'Missa solemnis', the Ninth Symphony, the Verdi 'Requiem' and the Monteverdi 'Vespers', have each had several performances, with 'Gerontius', the Mozart C minor Mass, and other works sometimes. In 1978 the Mozart 'Requiem' was sung in memory of Alan Richards, leader at Music Camp for so many years: and in 1980 saw the biggest gathering hitherto – the Berlioz 'Grand Messe des Morts', with some 270 performers.

A happy occasion was the celebration of the 100th Camp in 1981, for which Margaret Montgomery wrote a short history, more detailed than the present account. For the first part of the week a fairly normal programme was rehearsed and performed, including the first recent performance of Handel's 'Occasional' Oratorio, edited by Merlin Channon, and works by several Music Camp composers – Edric Cundell, Anthony Pople and Arnold Cooke. For the final weekend, many old friends appeared, making a total of over 300 on the site; John Gardner conducted his 'A Te Deum for Pigotts', a new work commissioned for the occasion; Roger Norrington conducted the Mozart 'Requiem' and the Vaughan Williams 'Serenade to Music'; and I conducted the Verdi 'Requiem' and the Beethoven Ninth Symphony, as a concluding thanksgiving for the fifty-four years of music which so many of us had experienced together.

In 1978 a charitable Company was formed, 'Music Camp Limited', to act as a holding company to own legally the Music Camp property, and to give some financial stability for future developments. Whereas in the first few years Camp had no possessions, and borrowed or hired a minimum of equipment, nowadays it owns kitchen gear, furniture, musical instruments, and a valuable library of choral and orchestral music, founded in memory of my wife Elizabeth. The Company has a wide charter for its activities; besides assisting music at Pigotts as its original purpose, it is extending its interest in other ways for the support of amateur music as a whole.

Someone who has never visited Pigotts may wonder at the persistence of the 'camping' feature and the extent of amateur building and maintenance which I have stressed. To my mind, these features are very important and have had a large share in the continued vigour of Music Camp. Originally adopted for economy's sake, in these more luxurious times they are valuable for other reasons. An 'al fresco' existence (if this term is still valid for some of the luxurious caravans which appear at Pigotts), for a week together in a beautiful country spot, cut off from normal distractions, produces a corporate feeling and a concentration on a common purpose – music and friendship. The slight discomforts – typified by the word 'Elsan' rather than 'W.C.' – maintain a useful bias towards youth as the years go by. It is understood that everyone must live on the site, taking a full share in the daily chores, and not being absent without good reason; and there comes a time when the old and valued friend becomes an occasional visitor and gives place to someone younger. Also the opportunity to learn and display skills other than musical ones is welcome to many; there are in fact several people who are as keen to come to 'working parties' as to parties where music is the prime purpose. And there are many who can enjoy walking around and saying 'I built that bit of wall and repaired that windowframe years ago' – the wall may not be very straight, or the woodwork roughly done, but there is a sense of ownership in the result.

The Music Camp has been very fortunate in the quality of its membership. Many of the pre-War enthusiasts went on coming till old age prevented them, and still showed that they were among the best amateurs around; there were many professionals who took the Camp as their annual holiday, and close connections were maintained with the Universities and, at some periods, with the Colleges of Music. It is interesting to read the references to Music Camp given in two autobiographies (David Franklin and David Higham refs 15 & 23). Years ago I gave up keeping an accurate list of all who had attended Music Camp, but it already contained some 2,500 entries. Twenty years ago there were few of the big orchestras which did not contain a few Camp names; the Richards, Walton brothers, Peter Beavan, Jack Brymer, Fritz Spiegl, Alan Hyde, Leonard Friedman, the two Brains, come to mind; and among the singers, Steuart Wilson, April Cantelo, John Shirley-Quirk, John Noble, David Franklin, and Maureen Lehane. A list of conductors appears in the 100th Camp booklet already mentioned; here we probably owe most to Edric Cundell, Colin Davis, Roger Norrington, John Gardner and Nicholas Braithwaite. An analysis of the professional occupations of the amateur members of Camp would be interesting; I would expect to find a bias towards the scientific/mathematical intelligence, with three Fellows of the Royal Society as a start; there are many teachers of music and of other things; and there would be a notable shortage of the wealthy and of keen business types!

Music Camp has in general avoided publicity, from which it could derive no advantage; the independence from outside audiences, though removing the excitement of public performance, has removed also the financial burden from which so many of the larger amateur societies suffer.

I no doubt am prejudiced, but I always feel, when facing a typical Music Camp gathering, that probably there exists nowhere else so talented a body of singers and players, not specially collected for a particular performance, which can competently read through a Mozart Mass, a Bruckner 'Te Deum', perhaps even a 'Symphony of Psalms' – this is not to suggest that the Camp spends most of its time in reading such things through, which it would in fact seriously rehearse, but just that it musters an unusually high degree of musical skill. At the last Reunion (1984/1985), when the work for performance was the Verdi 'Requiem', and there were some 260 performers in all, I asked for a show of hands, and roughly counted 20 who were doing this work for the first time; the very large majority had done it three times or more; and there were 50 who had done it ten times or more.

I have given more space to detail about the Music Camp in this book than to other enterprises, partly because I know more about it than about some others, but also because of its unusual features, which seem to me to be:

(a) the completeness of its amateur approach to music;
(b) the temporary isolation from the outside world during the major Camps, giving concentration and producing a tolerant and happy community;
(c) the tradition of 'giving a hand' – from potato-peeling to addressing envelopes – at whatever needs to be done.

I think that most people come to Music Camp as anxious to contribute to its welfare as to derive benefits for themselves, and in this atmosphere conceit and selfishness do not flourish.

I also think that Music Camp has made an appreciable and detectable effect on the general improvement and better standards in amateur music which have occurred in this country during my lifetime.

3
Some Other Organizations

Introduction

I hope that what I have written so far does not suggest that I think good amateur music is to be found only at Music Camp! I shall be coming later to the vast field of Chamber Music, to some amateurs the most rewarding of all; but this Chapter is about the choral/ orchestral societies, of which the NFMS handbook lists nearly 800 as giving public concerts with amateur performers – an activity outside the normal scope of Music Camp, but in which many of my friends are prominent. So great is the variety in the size, purpose and accomplishment of such music that I can think of no exactly logical arrangement.

In Section A I pick out three societies which give performances of remarkably high standard – I believe as high as can be regularly obtained by a fully amateur group. These are the Chelsea Opera Group, the Salomon Orchestra and the Hertfordshire Chamber Orchestra. The two first were closely linked with Music Camp at the time of their formation, and these links of common membership are still strong. The Hertfordshire Orchestra started later, but also has many players who are members of Music Camp. The three have much in common – they use professional conductors, and soloists also when needed, though the fees paid are not in the most expensive bracket; they do not meet weekly, but arrange concentrated rehearsals for each concert; they have a fairly ruthless attitude to membership – an unreliable attender or an indifferent performer is not likely to be asked again. Their finances depend on ticket receipts, occasional payment for the orchestra's services, benefactions and grants. And most important, their performances are worth listening to.

Section B describes some well-established choral societies where I have some personal contacts – Wells, Ipswich, Woking, Newcastle and Edinburgh. The typical routine is to give two or three concerts a year, with weekly choral rehearsals, sometimes using a professional orchestra, sometimes a local group stiffened with professionals if necessary; there is usually a strong local tradition of support.

Finances are often difficult, particularly if a large proportion of income goes in professional fees.

In Section C I refer very briefly to a few amateur orchestras – a tiny cross-section only; Ealing, Kensington, Bristol, Edinburgh, Oaks Farm (the latter is anomalous in this Chapter, in that it did not give concerts).

In Section D are some smaller choral groups. Here there is a big variation in size and purpose; from the Renaissance Singers and London Orpheus, to small groups of perhaps only 20 singers, often with a high standard and a specialist approach.

Section E I can only describe as 'miscellaneous', though certainly in no derogatory sense: the Manchester 'Double-Fisters', the W11 Children's Opera Group, and Haddo House for example.

Finally in Section F are two institutions and three rare occasions: the music of Guys Hospital and of Imperial College, where there is naturally a continual change of youthful membership. 'Fidelio', the first staged opera at Music Camp, an unusual 'Messiah' in the Albert Hall, and a 'St Matthew Passion' in a German prisoner-of-war camp.

SECTION A

Chelsea Opera Group

The Chelsea Opera Group started in 1950, mainly from the enthusiasm of three people – Stephen Gray and Colin Davis, already well known at Music Camp as oboist and clarinettist respectively, and David Cairns, general musician and critic, who has referred to the Group as 'a crystallization of the Mozart fervour which gripped Oxford after the War.' The idea of giving a concert version of 'Don Giovanni' in the Oxford Holywell Music Room (the oldest music room in Europe) in February 1950, proved most successful. The orchestra was collected by Stephen Gray from Music Camp members and from the Kalmar Orchestra, a small student group which flourished at the time, and was conducted by Colin Davis, whose quality as a conductor was already clear. I played in this orchestra myself, and can remember the feeling of excitement – few amateurs at that time can have had the chance of playing Mozart in those happy conditions. The Group went on to become a sort of 'Mozart Repertory Company' for a year or two, giving concerts at Oxford and at Cambridge. Beethoven was introduced to the repertoire at a

London performance of 'Fidelio' in 1953, and the list expanded with a 'Falstaff' in 1956 and thereafter to a comprehensive range of composers and operas.

From 1957 the Group began to provide an orchestra for productions of the John Lewis Partnership Musical Society; Colin's engagements no longer permitted him to remain the sole conductor, and others began to appear on the rostrum – Braithwaite, Sillem, Keefe, Norrington, Woolfenden, for example. The original 'ad hoc' choruses which had proved adequate in the early days were superseded in 'The Flying Dutchman' in 1958 by a regular team for the purpose; soloists, at first often amateur, were now chosen from young professionals, many of whom much increased their reputation and experience from these appearances. A look at the list of works, conductors and soloists over 30 years is impressive; the Group has gone a long way since that first 'Don Giovanni' at Oxford. But though it has managed to remain a close and friendly group of excellent players, through these years it has always aimed at large-scale performances, including some usual works of limited box-office appeal; and its traditions have sometimes borne heavily on the organizers, for the concerts have often produced a loss, with professional fees and heavy expenses on administration, advertising, etc; and it has often depended for financial balance on benefactors and sponsors, together with occasional engagements for which it provides an orchestra and receives a fee.

Salomon Orchestra

The Salomon Orchestra was founded by a group of young musicians, mainly from Cambridge, in 1963, largely stimulated by Nicholas Steinitz; the name came from the famous group of Haydn symphonies. Its chairman of a few years ago, Oliver Taylor, described it at an NFMS conference in 1980 as an 'Unusual experiment – a non-professional orchestra on lines that most societies would find rather unorthodox'. Its declared purpose is the public performance of orchestral works at the highest standard that amateurs can reach.

Three concert series are planned each year; each programme (with a maximum of 90 minutes' playing time, so that rehearsal is adequate), has a public performance, usually at St John's, Smith Square, a good but expensive venue. It is often repeated at schools, universities and music clubs, for a fee which goes to the orchestra funds. No player receives a fee; there is never any paid 'stiffening', and conductor and soloists receive a uniform nominal fee. The small Committee, all playing members, manages the Orchestra's affairs, each member taking a due share of the labours of administration, publicity etc. The orchestra is in effect chosen afresh after each concert series, by personal recommendation and invitation from the members, who also state their opinion on future programmes and conductors. Payment of a subscription does not entitle a member to play, and 'fixers' have discretion to sack players who are below standard. Rehearsals are concentrated – each programme has about eight rehearsals over two or three weeks, and players are expected to attend all rehearsals.

These clear-cut and essentially democratic rules produce a high standard of alertness and performance, and difficult works occur frequently in the programmes; also able young conductors are very ready to appear with the orchestra – Braithwaite, Andrew Davis, Rattle for example in recent years – as are good soloists.

Financially the Orchestra is in a better position than most, by reason of the modest amount paid in fees, the substantial receipts from performances, and efficient and economic administration.

Hertfordshire Chamber Orchestra

The Hertfordshire Chamber Orchestra was founded in 1966 by a group of ex-County Youth Orchestra players, most of whom were also at Cambridge, for Andrew Davis to conduct. He conducted for its first six years or so, but had to give it up when he moved to Glasgow as assistant conductor of the BBC Scottish Orchestra. After some difficulties in replacement, the orchestra was rebuilt by a small group of players and Howard Williams, who was conductor from 1974 till about 1980, when he also became too busy to serve regularly. In 1982 a very satisfactory arrangement was made with Edmon Colomer, under whose baton the orchestra seems now to be flourishing vigorously. Though he is a Spanish resident he can manage to conduct two series of rehearsals each year and also the foreign tours; guest conductors are engaged for the remaining concerts, and this provides continuity of musical direction and also variety.

There are usually about 30 strings and double wind, sometimes augmented to permit the larger works to be included e.g. Dvořák or Brahms. Rehearsals are held mainly at three residential weekends per year, normally with two concerts the following weekend; probably one in London and one in Hertfordshire. There are occasional 'one-off' concerts with rehearsals on the day, for a music club or choral society. No 'stiffening' is used; members pay their own expenses for rehearsal weekends and concerts; there is additional income from ticket sales and playing for choral societies (once or twice a year). Most of the money goes on costs of concerts. The rehearsal weekends are self-supporting. Hire of concert halls, printing, publicity, hire of music (this can be a very expensive matter) and working expenses are the chief items.

The orchestra is essentially a group of friends. Most of the wind players have been playing together for several years, and meet also in other orchestras. The string fixing is done by recommendation, and people who are not good enough (or not popular) are not asked again. As well as in its excellent conductors, the orchestra was for many years fortunate in its leader, a barrister in private life, but with earlier professional musical experience. Programmes are chosen by the conductor with a sub-committee – whose function is often to restrain the choice of works which might not please the orchestra as a whole! Choice is of course difficult, more so for an amateur than for a professional group. There must be a reasonable amount for everyone to play, to make their rehearsals worth while; so that unusual orchestrations have to be avoided, unless the whole programme can be built round them; some instruments are difficult to arrange for, or too expensive – maybe a piano for a concerto, for example.

The programmes are often adventurous and depend very much on the hard work of the volunteer organizers and fixers on the Committee; particularly as foreign tours are a considerable feature of the orchestra's work. In recent years there have been visits to Belgium, Spain and Greece, sometimes with involvement in Festivals of European Youth music. Little known works like Schoenberg's 2nd Chamber Symphony and Frank Martin's Concerto for 7 Wind Instruments have been performed.

Many good reasons hold together an orchestra like this; the prime one of course is the desire of members to play in good conditions under a good conductor and to a high standard; then also the advantages of a weekend's intensive rehearsal, not only musically but also in the chance to get to know people more closely (as at some Summer Schools, or at Music Camp); the consequent possibility for some to be regular members, even though they live at some distance; the feeling that the rehearsal may be as rewarding and exciting as the performance itself. There is a risk of conflict in the orchestra between the striving for higher standards and possibly more prestigious concerts, and the wishes of many for a more stable and secure membership, in which the claims of loyalty to long standing players may be more important to the general good than a marginal improvement from a few perhaps technically better players. This is an echo, at a higher level, or problems mentioned elsewhere in this book!

SECTION B

Wells Cathedral Oratorio Society

The present Society preserves traditions from the turn of the century, when groups from the music societies of Wedmore, Shepton Mallet and Wells itself occasionally met for performances directed by the Cathedral organist and choirmaster. Through two World Wars, conditions were not easy; but after 1946 it was more possible to think of joint programmes on a larger scale. In line with the generally improving standards in amateur music, professional singers began to be engaged as soloists; the orchestra was mainly local in origin, till 1978 when a fully professional team was used. The records of those years give a pleasant impression of cooperative effort among the original three societies, which of course involved considerable travelling for rehearsals, etc. in those days when the provision of a special train might be the best way of moving a choir or an audience from Point A to Point B! The magnificence of Wells Cathedral as a home for great music, and the professional skills of the Cathedral organist and his staff, were important in keeping these societies together through many vicissitudes.

Now in the 1980s the Cathedral Oratorio Society has a season running from September until April, with weekly rehearsals at the three centres, Wells, Shepton Mallet and Wedmore. There are two main concerts and a Carol Concert, the latter being run separately from a financial point of view, and its profits going to charity. No visitors are invited to take part in the singing, though sections of the Cathedral Choir sometimes assist. There is a chorus of 180–200 at concerts; there is no audition at the present time, but this is a subject for annual discussion and debate, and it might become necessary in the future to restrict membership. Costs are rising steadily, and the proportion of the annual income which goes in professional fees is very high.

Ipswich Bach Choir

In April 1928 the organist and choirmaster of St Mary-le-Tower in Ipswich performed the Bach 'St Matthew Passion' with his church choir. This was very successful, and led to cooperation with others and eventually to the formation of the Ipswich Bach Choir, which became a full-scale Society with an impressive record of performances – by its Jubilee in 1979, the 'St Matthew Passion' had been performed 31 times, the 'St John' 15, and the B minor Mass 13 times.

Though in the earlier days the Choir had the advantage of several amateur soloists of distinction, the financial side was always an anxious one; in the fifties, the choir might well have collapsed for this reason; to quote an active Secretary at that time 'In these days, even a small professional orchestra may cost about £100, and professional soloists not less than an average of £15, often very much more'. There were at that time no grants from public bodies, and losses on concerts were sometimes made good by the conductor and his friends.

At the present time, the conductor is Merlin Channon, well known in Music Camp circles; the choir numbers about 100 and rehearses weekly. Two concerts are usually given each year, and the choir is not augmented; the orchestra is assembled from local amateurs of good standard, with occasionally some 'stiffening'. Newcomers are recruited by personal recommendation and also by advertisement; they have to pass an audition. I asked Merlin how he would describe the organization and main purpose of his Choir. He replied 'The policy and future programmes are determined by the Conductor and the Committee. Occasionally the Choir is asked for suggestions of works to be performed. The hard work is done by the Committee, who are elected annually. I maintain that the purpose of this Choir is for the study and performance of choral works of excellence. Subsidiary pleasures are to be had, too!' Merlin's interest in Handel's music has led him to produce a new edition of Handel's 'Occasional' Oratorio, which thus had its first modern performance at Ipswich in

1981, repeated at the Queen Elizabeth Hall in London in 1982 and at the Three Choirs Festival in 1983.

Woking Choral Society

This society is run by an old friend of mine, Nicholas Steinitz, who had been its conductor for many years. It illustrates the way in which the NFMS can help on the promotion of concerts, some of which would not be possible for a Society of this size with strictly local support.

There are some 140 singing members – Nicholas' estimate was that at an average rehearsal there was an 80% to 85% attendance. There are usually three concerts a year: two large-scale ones with orchestra, and one usually requiring less expensive accompaniment and suited to the Christ Church in Woking, which is good acoustically but has not enough space for a large occasion. The orchestral concerts have to be in Guildford Cathedral, a fine building but not too helpful to the sound. The orchestra used is basically amateur – it has a preliminary rehearsal in London and another on the day of the concert, for which the players receive an expense fee. Its members are invited personally by the conductor, who with the aid of a committee decides on programmes and organizes the detail of concert arrangements, and the engagement of professional soloists.

The concerts cover a variety of major works – recently for example there have been the Verdi 'Requiem', 'Christmas Oratorio', 'St John Passion', 'Dream of Gerontius'; but two recent performances were by agreement with the N.F.M.S. in line with their policy of special help on occasions when unusual modern works, or special expenditures, are involved. The first was Malcolm Williamson's 'Christ the King'; and the second, jointly with the Guildford Choral Society, was the Britten 'War Requiem'; for this latter occasion, a full professional orchestra was engaged, and the turnover was of the order of £13,000, with a packed Cathedral.

Newcastle-upon-Tyne Bach Society

The Newcastle-upon-Tyne Bach Society is a good example of a moderate-sized chorus group, well established and with a fine tradition. It was founded in 1915 by W. G. Whittaker, and was one of the earliest regional Bach Choirs (there are 29 Bach Choirs in the British Isles, and probably only the London (1876) and Edinburgh (1888) pre-date it). Whittaker wanted particularly to explore the Bach Cantatas with a small highly-trained choir approximating in size to Bach's forces; in 1920 he gave a complete 'St Matthew Passion' with 40 singers and 26 players. Several first performances of the works of Holst and Vaughan Williams were given by the choir, and the first revivals of the Byrd 'Great Service' and the Tallis 40-part Motet were also to their credit.

There has always been close connection with the Music Faculty of the University, where its conductor now for several years, Percy Lovell, is Senior Lecturer. It is kept to a size of 100 voices; there is sometimes (as with so many societies) a shortage of men, but in general there is no problem of recruitment, which is by audition (and tactful suggestion for retirement where necessary). Rehearsals and most concerts are in King's Hall, the main hall of the University; seating 400, with good acoustics; for larger programmes, churches or the Cathedral are used. A few students pass through the chorus, but for the most part the singers are a stable and genuinely amateur body. Soloists are professional or regional semi-professional.

The Society works closely with the Tyneside Chamber Orchestra, a string orchestra of 25 players, mostly talented amateurs of the district, with additional wind when needed; this orchestra also is directed by Percy Lovell. A smaller group, the Camerata Singers, of 25 voices, is chosen from the Society and from the University Madrigal Choir; it has its own schedule of engagements, and its repertoire is heavily based on 16th- and 17th-century music. There are several other amateur performing groups in and around Newcastle, so that the keen amateur is well provided for in this area.

Edinburgh Royal Choral Union

The Edinburgh Royal Choral Union has a proud history. Founded in 1858, for many years it stimulated and provided orchestral and choral concerts of major works, at a time when such music was rare in Scotland. Later it had the credit of the first performance in Scotland of 'Gerontius' (1903), the B minor Mass (1907) and Britten's 'War Requiem' (1964). The title 'Royal' was granted in 1911. The E.R.C.U. had a large share in the opening years of the Edinburgh Festival, before the formation of the Festival Choir.

At present it gives three concerts each year in the Usher Hall, including a very popular 'Messiah' on New Year's Day. There are rehearsals all through the season, with auditions for new members, and for all singers triennially. A singer will not be allowed to take part in the concerts without a good attendance record. A Committee of Directors is elected annually; the Committee determines the choice of programme, but of course takes note of the opinions of the chorus master and of the members in general. Conductor, soloists and orchestra are professional; and the rapidly rising costs in this direction are making it very difficult to continue the pattern of music-making which has been possible so far. Fund-raising projects and further sponsorship must be sought out and developed.

SECTION C

Ealing Symphony Orchestra

The Ealing Symphony Orchestra is an example of a moderate-sized local orchestra, with no pretensions to ambitious programmes or large expenditure, but providing its members with the pleasures of steady weekly rehearsals with an occasional concert mainly to local audiences. It was founded in 1921 as the Hanwell Orchestral Society; originally without outside support, it was affiliated in 1961 to the Ealing Technical College as an evening class, until 1981 when it became independent once again. There were occasional problems when the Technical College was in formal control e.g. when it was difficult to exclude some players of poor technical standard. Now, however, the organization is by committee, the secretary doing as usual most of the hard work. There were (1982) about 40 subscribing members, and membership is pretty stable; a few friendly professionals join in for concerts, but are not allowed to oust regular fee-paying members.

Rehearsals are weekly during term at the Technical College; there will be three or four concerts a year, usually in local churches, and sometimes joining with local choral societies. There may be a grant, e.g. from the G.L.C., for unusual expenses such as a particular soloist, or a piano. In effect, enough money is raised by programme sales, benefactions, etc. to cover the extra expenses of giving a concert.

Programmes and policy are democratically debated; but, in the words of one member, 'in the absence of a knowledgeable benevolent dictator, the putting together of programmes can be a terrible fat-chewing occupation for the Committee; the problems include difficulty of the music in relation to rehearsal time, use of awkward instruments, availability of music, popularity of music with players and audience, etc.' – all well-known problems to some of us!

Amateur orchestras, particularly in London, are legion; there is a good deal of change and overlapping in membership; Simon Routh points out later in the book that a good and keen player in London can if he wishes book himself twice over for every night in the week. One of the pleasant features of such playing is, of course, the near-certainty of meeting some friends in any group, whatever its name.

Kensington Symphony Orchestra

One remarkable orchestra must be mentioned, the Kensington Symphony Orchestra inspired and conducted by Leslie Head, with its associated operatic group, Pro Opera. This has been running for some 25 years, and its record of performances, all by a mixed group of amateurs and students, is most impressive. Its policy seems to have been to tackle anything however big and unknown, and to bring it to performance. Major works of Berlioz, Britten, Donizetti, Mahler, Strauss, Verdi, some unknown to the ordinary audience, some in fully staged form, and in particular the works of Bax and of Havergal Brian, are on the record. The enthusiasm of Leslie Head and of some of his helpers, like Lewis Foreman and Shirley Karney, has evidently triumphed over the many obvious difficulties. I know nothing of the finances of this orchestra, but I suspect that private generosity, in labour even more than in cash, must have had a large part to play in its success.

Bristol Chamber Orchestra

I include a few lines about the Bristol Chamber Orchestra largely because when I asked the Secretary in general terms what he thought was the main purpose of the Orchestra, he replied proudly 'To give pleasure to others, to remain independent, and to pay our way.' This is a small organization, about 20 years old, founded and inspired by keen amateurs; a nucleus of about 26 strings, with wind and brass added as needed for perhaps two concerts a year. The members' subscription covers the hire of rehearsal rooms, and it is clear that there are hardly any administrative expenses – one infers a very devoted group which runs the Orchestra, which is independent of subsidy or other commitment.

Edinburgh Symphony Orchestra

The Edinburgh Symphony Orchestra is a little larger, and gives the same impression of efficient administration and independence. About 20 years old, it has some 30 strings and full wind as needed; it gives three concerts a year, with weekly rehearsals through the season. Auditions are given to all, and regular attendance demanded; no 'stiffeners' are included for concerts, and no fees are paid, apart from a small honorarium to conductor and secretary. Recruitment is largely through personal contacts, and programmes (mainly 18th- and 19th-century music) decided by the conductor, with advice from the Committee. Income is mostly from members' subscriptions and from ticket sales; a recently-formed society – 'Friends of the E.S.O.' – has its own programme of meetings and musical evenings, and helps financially e.g. in the purchase of orchestral music. Expenses are almost all on hiring halls, printing and advertising, and music hire.

Two or three members of Music Camp are in this Orchestra, and I formed the impression that its success is due to the sensible attitude to discipline and rehearsals and to the emphasis on friendship and sociability. Economy in expenditure and 'overheads' has resulted in a credit balance for the two seasons for which I saw the balance-sheet.

Oaks Farm Orchestra

The Oaks Farm Orchestra was a remarkable one-woman effort which lasted for 65 years. Mrs Crump, in 1911 an oboe student at Guildhall School of Music, felt that there was little opportunity for students and their friends to practise sight-reading and to learn the orchestral repertoire, and she started a series of weekly meetings for this purpose. Everything was very informal; she conducted; the group thus started held together during the First World War, and played occasionally at concerts.

After the War, meetings continued; this lady married an amateur 'cellist, and they bought a small farm near Croydon which had a large barn which could be converted for rehearsal use – large enough, but not so large as to be tempting to expand into concert-giving. Whenever she could, Mrs Crump bought orchestral music and built up an extensive library; also she acquired 'difficult' instruments such as double-basses, which suitable people might be encouraged to learn as second- or third-study instruments.

So a tradition was built up, that there was always music at Oaks Farm on Sunday afternoons, with hardly an exception for many years. Anyone who was keen and reasonably proficient might seek an invitation and turn up. Possible redundancies in the wind departments were avoided by discreet mutual arrangements among the 'regulars'; the programme was chosen each week to suit the attendance. For many years the hostess was also the conductor; as the occasion arose, young conductors needing the experience took over the baton. Her daughter, a professional horn-player, was a link with oncoming young students.

Mrs Crump died in her eighties, leaving behind her an enviable record of the promotion of music and friendship among what must have been several thousands of people in this long stretch of years.

SECTION D

Smaller groups of singers have a variety as great as that of orchestras. Many, of course, have no special thought of performance, and are merely extended madrigal or part-song groups, open to anyone who is keen to join in – particularly tenors! But some are more selective, aiming at a higher standard of singing, perhaps with some speciality, e.g. baroque or unaccompanied music, and giving occasional performances. The standard of some may be difficult to distinguish from that of a professional performance, and there is always the possibility of a formal changeover from amateur to professional, sometimes imposed by the difficulties raised by the unions (Musicians' Union or Equity), and perhaps also in order to enhance the conductor's professional reputation.

Renaissance Singers

A group which has remained amateur through most of its history is the Renaissance Singers, started in 1944 particularly to perform Renaissance music. For a time it had no serious rivals in this field, and was able to choose its 20 singers from the best amateurs in London. It had many B.B.C. appearances, made records of such works as the Vaughan Williams Mass in G minor, and took part in various grand occasions, such as an Easter concert in St Paul's Cathedral and some National Trust programmes in 'stately homes'. An excellent and personal account of its early years, under the conductorship of Michael Howard, is given in David Higham's book (Ref. 23). At a later period its conductor was Richard Barnes, well-known at Music Camp as conductor and keyboard player. In the sixties it began to lose its special position, as there were now many other small groups competing for good singers; nevertheless it still maintains a good reputation. It operates nowadays as an I.L.E.A. evening class.

London Orpheus Choir

The London Orpheus Choir was founded in 1945 and was the first amateur choir to perform at the Queen Elizabeth Hall, then newly opened; there it gives about four concerts a year, which fit in with other programmes already planned for the Hall, and will usually include an element of modernity. It is at present about 80 strong and has regular auditions for membership. For many years it operated nominally as an I.L.E.A. evening class, thus having the advantages of comfortable rehearsal quarters at the City Literary Institute. In recent years, however, the rise in I.L.E.A. fees and the insistence on 'residential' qualifications for such rehearsals disturbed these happy arrangements, though I believe that they have to some extent been restored recently. Michael Crombie, known at Pigotts for being in charge of musical youngsters from Wanstead High School, is the accompanist and deputy conductor of the Choir.

The Choir has given many performances and broadcasts of major works; e.g. the B minor Mass and various Bach cantatas, Mozart's C minor Mass; some works have been commissioned from modern composers; a complete performance of the 'Messiah' and one of 'Semele' form part of the Handel tercentenary celebrations for 1985.

For most of the Choir's concerts, a small professional orchestra is used.

Coro Capella

As a smaller specialist group, Andrew van der Beek founded the Coro Capella in 1977. He writes, 'I first felt the need for such a choir at a time when I was very excited by the sound of cornetts and sackbuts and all those weird and wonderful Renaissance instruments. I was running the London Cornett & Sackbut Ensemble and beginning to realize that all those intradas and canzonas do tire after a while, and that all the really great music of the 16th century was the sacred polyphony written for the grand cathedrals and courts. Luckily for me, it was the practice, especially in Europe and most especially in Spain, for wind players to join in with the singers on the more important feast days. So I planned a series of concerts of great Renaissance cathedral music, and as I was then a relatively young man full of ideas as to how a choir should sound, I formed a choir ad hoc. (Andrew goes on to describe the quality of voice which he looked for.) 'We don't meet regularly, but rehearse usually three times in the week before each concert, enough to get to know the music without tiring of it. I suppose one could say that the Coro Capella is not so much a choir as a list of people from amongst whom it is convened for each concert – we normally need more, or less, or certain voices – not much Renaissance music seems to be for S.A.T.B. Our median complement is 26.

'We don't audition; we are always trying out, in concerts, new singers recommended by existing members and others. We don't have any pros in the choir. I'm not sure that we need them, and anyway their trade union wouldn't allow it. Equity must be the only trade union that actively diminishes the amount of work available for its members. Soloists and instrumentalists, when we need them, are all professional.

'I agree that the financial side of amateur music making is fascinating. I would love to know how some choir conductors do it – I think there must be a lot of rich aunts around. On Coro Capella's first series of concerts in St Pancras Church I made a thumping great personal loss, even though the Greater London Arts Association chipped in with £500. Since then I have had to be more cunning, and wait for opportunities. These (i.e. for unusually favourable financial arrangements) do not come often, and undoubtedly Coro Capella would have disappeared were it not for our association with the music publishers specializing in Renaissance polyphony, Mapa Mundi, whose founder has taken the choir under his wing and become our principal guest conductor. As the sort of music published by Mapa Mundi is just what Coro Capella was founded to sing, it is a very happy association.

'Up till now we have thought that St John's, Smith Squire, was a very suitable venue for our concerts. But unless one does nothing but Monteverdi and the more spectacular works of Gabrieli, it's almost impossible to break even there with our sort of music. One has to spend £300 or £400 on press advertising even to half fill the place, £125 (at the last count) to hire it for the day, print a handbill, etc.

'For our last concert we decided to avoid all that expense: go to a good church in the City for next to nothing; print no publicity. The audience was invited from among our friends and followers. It worked; we got the full house we wanted plus a small and predictable deficit. The audience got a free concert and the church got quite a bit in a plate by the door from people who thought they owed somebody something.'

Carissimi Consort

The Carissimi Consort is still another small expert group of singers with a specialist approach; I have the details from Edward James, who is closely connected with the group. It was founded and directed by Alan Armstrong in 1977 and has about 18 singers. All concerts are fixed for particular voice requirements, so that membership may change on occasions, round a fairly constant nucleus. Thus there are often more tenors than sopranos, and male alto parts are sung by male singers to give the right tone quality. Solo work is done by the choir members. On the average there will be eight concerts a year, each with three rehearsals. At a typical concert, probably somewhere near London, and arising from an invitation from the local church group of one of the members, the performance will be on a Saturday evening, the singers will stay with local friends for the night, and will take part in the morning service on the Sunday. All proceeds will go to charity; occasional instrumentalists will collaborate when needed by the programme, which is normally of Baroque music, with emphasis on Monterverdi and Schutz. All fixing and programme decisions are by the conductor; there are no financial problems, no committee; the whole is totally undemocratic!

Suffolk Occasional Choir

The Suffolk Occasional Choir is an unusual group, organized over the past 20 years by a distinguished member of the Bar, Christopher Lubbock, who lives in Suffolk. Originally it was a small party of singers who were prepared to go along to help in the Sunday services of some church in the district which might like to have, on occasion, a more elaborate choral service than normal, e.g. a Cathedral-type setting of the anthems and responses. This proved a popular idea, and the group found themselves busy with music of increasing elaboration (usually unaccompanied, or voices with organ). Eventually, on one or two occasions in the year, a full performance of a major work with orchestra became a regular feature; either a performance on its own to which an audience was invited, or a performance forming part of a shortened Evensong. Many of the larger works so arranged in recent years were in the lovely church of Stoke-by-Nayland, outstanding in its position and dimensions, and particularly good for sound. The list of works performed here over a few years is impressive – Verdi 'Requiem', Monteverdi 'Vespers', even the Berlioz 'Grand Mass'; I had the pleasure myself of conducting the Beethoven Ninth Symphony and the Verdi 'Te Deum'. But of course the trouble and expense of arranging for such works, even with people who knew them very well, became rather prohibitive; and more recently works of the size of the Mozart or Fauré 'Requiems' have been the rule, and churches or halls which for various reasons were more easy to manage have been used.

For the smaller church services, the invited choir might be of 30 to 40 voices; for larger works, it was sometimes up to 100, with orchestra of 50 or more. About 90% of the performers came from the London area; fees were not paid to anyone; the expenses (mainly food) were covered, not always adequately, by a levy on the singers. Rehearsal would start in the morning (say immediately after the morning service) and continue through the afternoon. For one or two of the larger occasions, a rehearsal was fixed also for the Saturday evening, but this gave big problems in fixing accommodation, etc.

The circular letters which summon this Choir have (as one might expect from their origin) an inimitable clarity and forceful style. In particular, reference is often made in them to an (imaginary) character called 'Henrietta', who can always be trusted to do the wrong thing and to cause delay and confusion. One circular however was open to misinterpretation; it stated that 'ladies may wear trousers, gentlemen need not wear suits'. This prompted my wife Elizabeth (who was a pretty hand with a pencil) to draw a cartoon of the Choir at rehearsal, the gents without suits, the ladies wearing trousers – only.

SECTION E

Manchester and the 'Double-Fisters'

Before the War, I heard quite a lot about amateur music in Manchester, from various early members of Music Camp; and I was invited on one occasion to go myself to play in the 'Double Fisters' orchestra, accompanying Carl Fuchs in the Dvořák Cello Concerto. Philip Lewis, a dentist, also first clarinet at early Music Camps, and an energetic organizer of music, describes the orchestra thus:

'I was at Manchester Grammar School from 1914 to 1921, and at this school there was no "official" music whatsoever; music depended on there being a few interested masters who, out of school hours, ran an orchestra (strings only) and a music study circle. Around 1925, largely at the instigation of Edgar Fuchs, we collected a group of 6 to 7 (piano and strings) and busted away at Haydn, Mozart and Beethoven symphonies. All male at first; females admitted in 1928, including Marjorie Kendrick (later Rushton) and Joyce Bond (later Camden). It was these piano-duet ensembles which were dubbed "Double-Fisters" by one of the 'cellists. In the late twenties we first hired a hall and expanded into a full orchestra. Archie Camden conducted us, and a brass section came along from Foden's Band, with Harry Mortimer as one of the trumpets – I think it was this that got him interested in orchestral playing; he subsequently joined the Hallé. The players were mainly amateur, but with quite a few young pros, including Frank Butterworth; we shared expenses for hire of hall and music, and it was usually 3/6 per head. After Archie left Manchester we had several different conductors, including Dr Heath from Barmouth, a very good amateur. We did quite a lot of proper chamber music, and played several times at the Alderley Edge Festival. I am still concerned with this Festival, and notice with regret that adult entries in the chamber music classes are nowadays almost non-existent.'

(Edgar Fuchs points out that the Double-Fisters, in whose formation he takes much pride, was as far as he knows, the earliest obvious contact between the separate worlds of brass bands, amateurs and young professionals).

The W. 11 Children's Opera Group

Serena Hughes (closely connected, through brother and husband, with my orchestra, the 'Informals' in the 50s) was I believe the inspiring spirit in the formation of this Group in 1972 by enthusiastic parents who wished to provide their children, living in the W. 11 district of London, with a chance to take part in an operatic production. This enterprise has continued since then, with great success. The cast usually employs about 100 children, between the ages of 8 and 18. Since there are very few published operas which are suitable for performance in church by such a large cast of children, the Group has found it necessary, almost from the start, to commission new works – no less than 6 since 1972, including John Gardner's 'Bel and the Dragon', Stephen Oliver's 'The Girl and the Unicorn', and Timothy Kraemer's 'Jonah'.

The cost of commissioning is a major expense, which has risen very steeply (£40 in 1972 has become £850 ten years later). The costs of production (lighting, design, costumes, etc.) have been largely met by box office receipts, together with a subscription from each child taking part (£6 per head in 1981). Assistance in mounting productions has been freely given by parents and friends; a number of professional musicians who have played in the orchestra have given their services freely, and Nicholas Kraemer, the conductor throughout the series, has been most generous with his time in rehearsal and performance. Until 1980 a charitable trust covered the cost of commissioning and any overall deficit. This is no longer possible, so that the Group is enlisting the help of a body of Friends, and seeking other benefactions in order to keep this enterprise going.

Serena Hughes writes 'My role now as rehearsal pianist is infinitely simpler than when I was general slave and organizer! Costs have absolutely zoomed since our early days 12 years ago – then, with one grant of only £500 a year from a charitable trust, we still made a profit of a few hundred which we gave to the church. It's all got much more streamlined and professional now – more people are paid, lighting and costumes are ambitious, more staging construction! But there is still a lot of devoted time and work given free by talented professional parents and friends – otherwise of course it would never happen.'

Though I have never seen one of these operas myself, I am told that they are splendidly successful, and so many of my friends have a share in them that I feel they have a place in this book.

Haddo House

One of the pleasures that has arisen from the writing of this book is that I had an invitation, through my old friend Bernard Brown, to see what went on at *Haddo House*. (Alas, Bernard, so well known and loved by all his friends, was killed a few months after our visit, in a quite unnecessary riding accident.)

I had heard from many other friends of the special qualities of this centre of music in Scotland, and I was delighted when I came to join the orchestra for a performance of 'Gerontius' to find so many old friends there too – Eileen Lawrence leading the 'cellos, Anne Mines and Kay Hurwitz in the violas, and Wolf Moser in the chorus – I was able to arrange to stay a night with him in Aberdeen on the way home.

Take a historic house (now a National Trust property) 20 miles north of Aberdeen, with a wooden 'hall' of excellent acoustics near by; large enough for a chorus of 100, orchestra of 60, and audience of 400 I suppose; with an orchestra of very high standard, a disciplined and effective chorus, and soloists of the highest quality (Janet Baker, Neil Jenkins, Brian Rayner Cook); add a hostess-conductor, obviously loved by all; and the result was a memorable and most enjoyable performance.

Over the past thirty-five years June Gordon, now the widowed Lady Aberdeen, has built up a remarkable enterprise, a group of friends with a tradition of choral music, opera and drama. After the War, she and her husband were determined to have music in the special background of their home, remote through this may have seemed as a venue for large-scale music. But she was a musician trained at the R.C.M. and with a family tradition of enterprise. They started quite humbly with a local group, singing carols and the like; but hard work and regular rehearsal began to collect others from some distance round, and in 1947 'Messiah' was proposed, against opposition from some of the choir, who thought it too difficult. (Years later, the Verdi 'Requiem' was also opposed, as smacking of Popery.) But persuasion and persistence prevailed; the 'St Matthew' in 1950, the 'B minor' in 1953, 'Gerontius' in 1957, and thereafter a growing stream of major works showed that almost anything was possible. Distinguished soloists appeared, and came again as friends; Vaughan Williams personally encouraged June Gordon to conduct his 'Sea Symphony', and Britten conducted his 'Spring Symphony' in 1960. The orchestra was sometimes wholly professional, sometimes based on good amateurs who were ready to travel considerable distances for such happy music. On special occasions there were collaborations with festival bodies, and concerts in Aberdeen. Twice the 'Apostles' and 'Kingdom' were performed on successive days, as their composer had originally wished.

But this record of major choral works describes only a small part of what happens at Haddo. Both the drama (mainly Shakespeare) and staged opera (half a dozen of the Gilbert & Sullivan operas, 'Carmen', 'Fledermaus', Verdi's 'Macbeth' and 'Nabucco') appear – usually one theatrical, one opera and one musical performance each year. (Wolf Moser thinks that he is the only 'Nabucco' soloist who has ever made his entry on a real live horse!) The total labour that must go into fashioning an opera house or a Shakespearean stage from what is basically just a large village hall, must be immense; and Haddo must be geared the whole year round to rehearsals and preparations for these programmes. In addition there is now a junior choral society, with weekly rehearsals and an annual concert, which supplies young singers to the older chorus.

It was not my place to enquire how all this was financed; but the impression was not at all that of a wealthy patroness dispensing funds, but rather of many distinguished people contributing what they could to help the enterprise. I believe that there have been generous sponsorships and contributions from local industry, which feels pride in the musical reputation of this part of Scotland; I heard talk of a new Steinway grand piano, and of funds to re-roof the hall, when dangerous rot had been discovered. I imagine that most of the professionals come at their own expense or at nominal fees. Hospitality is generous, the large house is filled with guests, excellent food and drink were available to performers and friends in the impressive library, lined with portraits and heirlooms. Even to the first-time visitor like myself, there was a delightful and special atmosphere at

Haddo – a touch perhaps of Glyndebourne before the War, and more than a touch of Music Camp in that one felt that carpenters, cooks, stagehands and washers-up were all around, working happily for the good of Haddo and in tribute to its mistress, who was described to me by someone as 'the most difficult person I know to say "no" to.'

SECTION F

A music society associated with a hospital or university has its own set of problems – finance for example may be comparatively easy with some official support, and rehearsal rooms may be no problem; but there will be a continual change of membership which could make standards uneven, and examinations will be more important than rehearsals.

Guy's Hospital

At Guy's Hospital there are good Music Camp contacts through the family of Soothill. John, Professor at the Hospital, was President of the Music Society when it re-established itself after the War, and his son Peter, medically qualifying at the Hospital, was its conductor during the past few years. The Society in 1947–50 was described to me as a small group of pretty good people, perhaps 60 in the chorus, covering all departments of the Hospital staff, with a few instrumentalists, and using help when needed from R.A.M. students. Its organization was a 'pseudo-democratic oligarchy' and I received a vivid account of the tactics used by the President at a general meeting to deal with impractical or unwelcome programme suggestions – from a full-scale performance of 'Belshazzar's Feast' from a long-haired earnest type, to a diet exclusively of Gilbert & Sullivan from the 'hearties'. In fact, during this period the programmes included 'Dido & Aeneas', 'Diocletian', and the 'St Matthew Passion'.

A generation later, Peter described the Society as having three elements – students, hospital staff, and friends. The students have the larger say in policy, and have more time available than the staff; much of the money needed comes from the Student Union funds (to which all students contribute) and also from their efforts in selling tickets and programmes. The abandonment of hospital boundaries allows the intriguing spectacle of a junior nurse sharing a copy with a Professor and tolerating criticism from a megalomaniac student conductor (this is Peter's description of himself!). The choir and orchestra meet once a week during the autumn and spring terms – experience has shown that examinations must take precedence in the summer. The Christmas concert is a performance of a large-scale work (Mozart and Fauré 'Requiems', the B minor Mass and parts of the 'Christmas Oratorio', for example) and for many years has been given in Southwark Cathedral, which is close at hand. The tradition of this concert and the splendour of the Cathedral produces a large audience each year and usually a little magic.

The Spring concert is in one of the halls in the Hospital, and is usually of shorter items in a more relaxed atmosphere. There are also lunch hour concerts by particularly good hospital performers and invited professionals, and various carol concerts.

Peter says, 'Exams, night shifts, 110-hour working weeks and being "on call" every third night, inevitably disrupt rehearsals and concerts. Many members are quite unable to attend for two weeks running, and a conductor has to accept some quite unfamiliar faces at a concert; many make great efforts to appear, but responsibilities to the patients have to come first. There is also a big variation in standard. A few members have been professional players before turning to a hospital job; others can hardly read music and are there mostly for the parties. It is the policy to accept anyone who is keen and who does not actually damage the sound, and of course many wind players can only be accepted in the chorus.

'A committee is duly elected at the beginning of each year, but in practice the conductor chooses and gets the music, the secretary advertises the dates of the first rehearsals, and to everyone's surprise a chorus and orchestra seem to arrive. As long as Guy's remains a community, and people enjoy making music together, there will be a Guy's Music Club! The social functions of the Club are vital, and visits to the pub after a rehearsal and parties after a concert swell the numbers in remarkable fashion.'

Imperial College

Imperial College (a major part of the University of London) is enlightened in its attitude to music, which it regards as a desirable part of education for the scientist and engineer. I have many links with the College – I did some teaching there for a time, and know well Eric Brown, a Professor in Engineering, who has been connected with Music Camp for many years. The College provides some secretarial assistance and a modest grant towards the cost of a series of weekly professional concerts, a student symphony orchestra, a chamber orchestra, a wind band, and a large student choir.

The Choir was formed in 1949, and since 1953 has been trained and conducted by Eric Brown. Performances were at first in a nearby hostel; then for some years in the Hall of the Royal College of Music; and since 1969 in the College's own Great Hall, whose admirable general facilities are sadly marred by regrettable acoustics for large musical performances.

There are weekly rehearsals during term, and two weekends of intensive rehearsal each year – one in November in a fine Elizabethan mansion in Kent, the other extending to three or four days at the Music Camp at Pigotts. There are no formal auditions for newcomers, but attendance at a high proportion of rehearsals is required of anyone singing at a concert, when, according to the time of year and the proximity of examinations, numbers will vary from 100 to 180 or more. Auditions are required however for membership of the Madrigal Singers, an *a capella* group whose members must all remain active in the main choir.

The Choir's performances have ranged from Monteverdi and Scarlatti to Honegger and Britten, and, included in the year before this was written, Handel's 'Dixit Dominus', Verdi's 'Requiem', and the 'St John Passion'. It is the Choir's intention that every undergraduate shall have the chance to sing either the B minor Mass or the St Matthew Passion during his college career, and these two works therefore alternate at three-year intervals in the programme.

The music is chosen by the conductor, the students having been invited to make suggestions. The Choir is managed however by a vigorous student committee, which handles finance, printing and publicity, membership (there is an annual subscription), the hiring of scores and parts, the sale of tickets, the transport of the Choir to weekend rehearsals, and general concert arrangements.

The orchestra for the Choir's concerts is separately enlisted for each performance, and consists largely of experienced amateurs, mostly from outside the College, with some semi-professional stiffening; moderate fees are paid to soloists; the conductor is of course unpaid!

Because of the connections with Imperial College, it is appropriate here to describe some unusual performances in Nairobi, Kenya.

Two members of the Imperial College Choir married, and ultimately settled in Kenya. When the Committee of the Music Society of Nairobi wished to give three performances of Haydn's 'Creation', they suggested that their old conductor, Eric Brown, might be persuaded to come for the occasion.

There is no regular professional music in Nairobi, but quite a lot by enthusiastic amateurs among the expatriate European community. There is a Music Society which runs a choir of 150 voices and an orchestra of some 40 players. (I have been told that this orchestra was originally started and conducted by another member of Music Camp, Bernard Lewis). Eric having accepted the invitation, thorough rehearsals began, so that by the time of his arrival the notes had been mastered. There were then concentrated rehearsals spread over ten days for orchestra, chorus and soloists, and then the performances in Nairobi Cathedral. The soloists, trained and experienced singers all, were Nairobi residents. The Cathedral is a fairly large building, of grey stone in a cruciform shape, and has pleasant acoustics; it was filled on three consecutive days by an appreciative audience.

The 'Creation' was so much enjoyed that Eric was invited to return in 1983 to conduct a more ambitious work, the Verdi 'Requiem'. When tactfully consulted the previous year as to whether local resources alone would be adequate for this, he had suggested that some orchestral leaders, and some of the soloists, would have to be imported. Someone had the inspired idea of tackling the Cultural Attaches variously present in Nairobi: an E.E.C. Nairobi Festival of Music would surely promote international goodwill! After some persuasive talk the general idea found favour; the Italians were keen – entirely at their own expense – to produce some soloists, the Dutch to provide a leader and another violinist from the Amsterdam Concertegebouw Orchestra, the French to send an oboist and a trumpeter, the Germans two more string players and the British a bassoonist. Seven first rate instrumentalists and three singers were thus 'subscribed'. There was still some official difficulty with the British Council over the expenses of Eric himself – after all, he was an amateur! In the end it was left to K.L.M., the Dutch airline, to provide his passage and to the local enthusiasts to provide his keep.

The Choir of the Nairobi Music Society was again excellent, and had been well prepared by a Nairobi resident. The Orchestra had to adjust to the addition of the European visitors, and worked strenuously for a week to do so. All problems were overcome: the minimum team of six trumpeters was assembled from far and near, a large bass drum was found in a school, borrowed and fitted with new skins, which were also found somewhere or other; the Italian soloists, unaccustomed to singing in so dry an atmosphere and at such an altitude (Nairobi is 6000 feet above sea level), came to terms with their misgivings. And to a crowded Cathedral the Verdi 'Requiem' received its first Kenyan performance. It was vociferously received, as was the second performance the next day, when the added confidence of experience led to a more polished and so of course to a more musical performance. When no performers are paid, but the audience pays for admission, a second concert is both possible and necessary – to meet the enormous cost of importing the sheet music from Britain. The improvement engendered by this second chance is something that British amateur societies can but envy.

The three occasions remaining now to be described have each some rather unusual features.

'Fidelio': The First Staged Opera at Music Camp

It is not usual to ask opera singers to be also useful wielders of pick and shovel – except perhaps in 'Fidelio', where Rocco's performance in this respect is often unconvincing. Not so at a performance of this opera at Music Camp in 1952, where the whole project started literally with the excavation of a pit (in hard clay and flints) big enough to take most of the strings of the orchestra. The hard labour of this digging (there was not room in the old agricultural barn where this took place for mechanical aids), together with the building of stage, scenery and audience seats, over the preceding months, was shared by all who took part.

We were very fortunate in the cast. Leonora was Elizabeth Abercrombie, a charming and lovely singer, experienced at Covent Garden, who inspired everyone. At rehearsal, I found myself once in tears as she sang the passage where she unlocks Florestan's fetters. Florestan was a craftsman from Nottingham; this was his first experience in serious opera; he had a marvellous voice for the part, and his acting developed through the rehearsals till at the end his performance was among the most convincing I have ever seen. The stage was a tiny one, and the scenery the simplest possible; by careful layout it was possible to seat an audience of 125 with good view of the stage. There were two performances, to a full house of invited guests.

Special wings were built to the stage to accommodate some of the wind players, and choral reinforcement for the Prisoners, for whom there was room on the stage for only about a dozen. The orchestra was led by Bessie Rawlins, an old friend of Music Camp from its earliest days.

The quality of the performance? The unusual mixture of 60 or 70 people, good amateurs and experienced professionals, isolated in a quiet country spot for a week, with no distractions and the sole purpose of performing a masterpiece to the best of their abilities and resources, was a memorable experience. Technically, the first flute of the orchestra, himself a regular Sadler's Wells player, described it as 'Sadler's Wells on a slightly off night.' Emotionally, Victor Gollancz, a most experienced and critical connoisseur of opera, referred to the performance in his book (ref. 18) as 'one of the most moving I have ever heard.'

'Messiah from Scratch'

'Stand up, the Chorus' – and the whole of the Albert Hall rose to its feet, or so it seemed to me, playing in a vast orchestra of some 250 players which filled the normal floor area. It was in December 1974, a performance which seems to have started something of a fashion in amateur music.

The idea of collecting a large amateur body, just to sing and play through the Messiah – no rehearsal, no audience in particular – apparently occurred to two scientists over lunch at Imperial College, London, both amateur players themselves, and both with ideas and interest in unusual organizations. They saw no reason why they should not attempt something of this kind – they might lose a little money, but they would have a lot of fun, and the organization of a concert seemed a lot simpler than the planning of an experiment in modern Physics. For such an idea, 'Messiah' was the obvious work – we all know and love it – and the Albert Hall the biggest and most convenient venue. So they walked across to the Hall forthwith, and booked it. This alone must have been no mean feat, to persuade the management that they were to be taken seriously! Back to Imperial College, to book a conductor – a fellow physicist whom they knew as the conductor of the student orchestra at the College. A fourth senior staff member was enlisted, to form a syndicate of four, the 'Tuesday

Partnership', to undertake the venture. If they could fill the Hall, it seemed even that a financial profit might result.

They were certainly inspired organizers. Publicity was effective and economical. The B.B.C. was persuaded to take an interest. Invitations and the distribution of tickets and seating arrangements were planned from first principles, with an amateur production-line of helpers, no professional agency being involved. A uniform charge of £1.25 was made, whether playing, singing, or listening. Applications arrived from everywhere to join in – choral coach parties were arranged from many distant points. The final publicity touch – a gift for a B.B.C. cameraman – was an excellent amateur trumpeter, who in fact had made or adapted his own trumpet, and was to be seen with a soldering-iron in use.

'On the Day' there was something of the atmosphere of a vast family party – no confusion, everyone had been told their place very efficiently, and was out to enjoy themselves. Many good friends were to be seen among the soloists and key players, organist, leader, etc.; for the solos, a smaller orchestra from those known to be the most experienced was used (this group had in fact had an optional rehearsal a couple of days earlier), but the main orchestra seemed to stretch as far as the eye could see, with a big body of assorted wind – no regard for the purist! – playing the Mozart accompaniments. Everyone who had asked to play or sing was allowed to do so; the total chorus attendance was 2,167, with a further 1800 who came to listen without singing.

The conductor – incredibly, his first experience of choral conducting – wisely did not attempt any particular finesse; but everyone knew the work, settled down quickly to a tempo, and put in some of the obvious expression marks. I must confess that I had accepted the original invitation to play myself largely out of musical curiosity – could such a large body of singers and players keep together, without rehearsal and with such big distances and confusing acoustics to make things even more difficult? The answer was that they did much more than just keep together – the music came through with remarkable effect, and some of the the climaxes were really exciting. Altogether a memorable party.

Since then, 'Messiah from Scratch' has been organized by the Tuesday Partnership many times, sometimes at Easter as well as Christmas; other works have been chosen – 'Elijah', Brahms 'Requiem', for example; and, more recently, Gilbert & Sullivan on occasion. But I believe that 'Messiah' is still the favourite choice, and the one most likely to fill the hall. The idea has been copied in various forms, and is I believe quite a money-spinner. The original conductor, Gavin Park, first clarinet in my orchestra for many years, said to me, 'I think this was the craziest thing I ever did', but he must have been very proud of the way things went; he wished only that old Handel could have been there too. A moral which he drew from the whole show, one very applicable to amateur music, was 'Don't pay other people to do something which you can do yourself, with sufficient effort.'

'St Matthew Passion' in Prison Camp

In Lent 1941 there was a performance of the 'St Matthew Passion' which surely must have been one of the most moving on record.

In the prison camp Oflag VII C, Laufen, near Salzburg, the idea grew of performing Bach's great work. There was difficulty in getting the music; but by the end of February a miniature score and four vocal scores had been obtained. A survey of available resources produced 28 choir singers, including a good tenor competent to sing the 'Evangelist'; an orchestra of six violins, one viola, three cellos, one bass, one flute, two clarinets, one horn and two pianists. There were two or three excellent general musicians who were prepared to spend the whole of their time till the performances (of which two were scheduled) in the necessary labours, which included translating and adapting the whole of the work, and copying the orchestral parts. Richard Wood (a professional singer, who most appropriately came to Music Camp after the war and sang the 'Minister' in our production of 'Fidelio' in 1952) was the conductor and inspirer of the whole.

He wrote, in an account of this enterprise, a few months later, 'It will be clear, I think, how well the St Matthew did fit the special conditions. First of all, the production of nearly any play or choral work could be ruled out at once because of the lack of female players. In the St Matthew however women soloists are not essential to the story and the crowd choruses could well be men's choruses – the soprano and alto parts are not essential dramatically; the interjaculating nature of the crowd choruses was suited to the choir's style; there are heaps of small parts and arias for different singers, and chorales in which the listeners could join; it was just within the capacity of the orchestra; and lastly, since the great majority of people in the Camp had never heard of it, they would not know what they were missing.

'... in making our version, we had a few guiding considerations; it must not be too long for Laufen listeners, who would not be likely to take easily to it; the essential story must stand intact; we must keep in enough of the arioso and arias to vary the recitative, since all the big choruses must inevitably go; and finally every number done must be within the range of a sincere and convincing interpretation, so that Bach should not come by too great an injustice.

'... The rehearsal sheet of a typical day was: 9.45 to 11.0, Christ part: 12.15 to 2.15. Orchestra: 3.00 to 4.00, choir: 5.00 to 6.00 solos: 8.00 to 9.00 small parts. The singer of the "Christ" part had never sung before he came here; I taught him every note by ear, his copy only muddled him since he could not read it! But his ear was good and after 5 weeks he knew it well and sang it at performance with forthright honesty of purpose. The choir learnt their parts quickly on the whole, and the orchestra also, though they found the accompanied recitatives difficult. The Narrator completely held the attention with his singing, which was always expressive, and at times really beautiful. The continuo player took time – he found the timing difficult. In the end we had a full day to spare.'

'... One pianist was used for recitative and solos, and the other for choruses (both for Barabbas!). Two violins and one viola made one orchestra, and flutes, clarinets and horn second orchestra, where two were necessary. The cellos and bass were divided. Horn took harmony parts in the choir chorales, tune in congregational chorales, and ordinary parts in the choruses. Since the instruments mostly double the voice parts in the choruses, there was never a part missing, though it might not be sung. A chief consideration was to save the tenor voices as much as possible: there was only one real tenor amongst them, and he without high notes! Another consideration was to keep in the most significant melody in whatever part Bach may have put it. One of the great points of interest lay in realizing how 'equal' Bach's parts are; no one is much more significant than another, and the music did not sound too bare when 8 vocal parts were reduced to 3 or 2.

'... Extra verses were added for all the congregational hymns (nos 16, 23, 44, 63). I was determined to have the audience-congregation singing (surely they sang some of the chorales in Bach's day?), so that they felt they were 'in', not just 'at', the performance. It was fine to have it so! ... When writing this account, I was very conscious again of the sense of adventure we had in learning and performing the work. The result seemed to me, at any rate, thoroughly efficient, sincere, convincing, and well, well, worth doing. It was also I believe for the performers and for most, if not all of the listeners, a real experience. The dramatic bits were dramatic; recitatives characteristic and well-timed, ariosi and arias "unphlegmatic" and well accompanied, chorus very good indeed and well supported by orchestra, and the chorales (except for no. 72) sung directly and at a good leg-stretch pace, which surely must have been one of their original purposes! I would like to think that Bach himself would have approved of the performances, under the circumstances.' On rereading his own account in 1982, Richard added the following: 'In spite of understandably strong anti-German sentiment in the Camp, I never doubted it was the right work to do then, given our resources; and I never heard anyone express doubts about it, either. We were congratulated by the senior German Camp Officer after one of the performances. I believe in the enterprise as much now as I did then, and in similar circumstances would not hesitate to do it again.'

4
The Amateur Society in Practice

Previous chapters have surveyed quite a variety of amateur music societies – from the venerable to the youthful, from annual budgets of £10,000 to £50, from committees with audited accounts to one-man dictatorships with no paperwork. As the astronomer describes the evolution of the universe from the extraordinary variety of stars and galaxies he can observe, so perhaps (on a somewhat different scale of magnitude!) we may compose the imaginary history of an amateur music group.

It may start round some particularly able enthusiast – perhaps a would-be conductor. He supplies the initial impetus and the hard work, and perhaps some local connections or a group of friends. Even with a small group, after a year or two he needs and attaches helpers for some of the unavoidable chores – fixing a rehearsal room, sending out circulars, 'chasing' the absentees, arranging for the music to be available, collecting subscriptions. After a little while these helpers become formally recognized, and their voices become important as growth proceeds – are there to be concerts, and if so, private to friends, or to the public? A larger room for rehearsals and concerts? Auditions or none? Is the musical standard to be raised? What scale of expenditure – are soloists, accompanists, the conductor, to be paid? Professional 'stiffeners' in the orchestra, perhaps even a fully professional accompaniment? By the time that these questions have been raised and answered, we have moved a long way from the original small circle of friends. Do we now adopt a formal constitution, seek financial support from outside, spent a lot of money in printing and advertising?

There is bound to be a traumatic period when the original conductor or mainstay of the organization comes to the end of his time – perhaps he is now too old or tired, perhaps the group now needs higher musical standards – or lower ones – for which he is not suited. Perhaps he is no longer popular with the group, too autocratic or too complaisant. Maybe the group collapses at this point; maybe it starts again with new management and with different social or musical aims.

Whatever stage a group has reached in this imaginary evolution (for which our astronomer could certainly find parallels!) it will have certain problems and needs in common; and the rest of this Chapter talks about them, based on my own experience and the conversation and advice of many good friends.

The Conductor

While a professional orchestra may sometimes feel that it could play through most of its programme without anyone on the rostrum, there is no doubt that an amateur group stands or falls by the quality of its conductor.

The perfect conductor for amateurs will of course be a paragon. No-one will doubt that he is the best musician around; he will be charming to all, but his authority will be unquestioned; he will have a witty remark for the right moment, and a cutting rebuke when it is deserved; he will know his score exceedingly well, and will have planned his rehearsals so that nothing is omitted, yet those who have little to do will not be kept inactive for long periods; he will know something about many of the performers, a number of whom will be his personal friends; his beat will always be clear, and his remarks few, but audible to everyone; disasters will not cast him down, and he will apparently enjoy himself throughout, but from time to time there will be moments of magic; and so on and so on.

Maybe this paragon does not exist. But anyone who does venture to conduct, even on a very humble level, must have self-confidence and must display some at least of the qualities described above. There is no substitute for experience (one reason why young would-be professionals should accept every opportunity of conducting, even a very bad team, where probably more is to be learnt than with an experienced one). Much can be learned from the criticism of one's friends, and there are of course many books on the subject of conducting (ref. e.g. 21) and training courses available to the amateur. I was told by one responsible for the organization of such courses that an obstacle to their success was the conceit of some, who felt that they had little to learn! Even at the amateur level, a good conductor of an orchestra must play a stringed instrument reasonably well, know something about the winds, and have a little experience at the back of an orchestra, counting bars. If he is conducting singers, he must have sung in choruses, and of course it is a great advantage if he has a pleasant voice and knows something about how to use it. It is a mistake to suppose that a professional musician of any kind is necessarily the best choice, if one is available; a typical organist-choirmaster for example may be a most unsuitable choice for an average amateur group.

A conductor of amateurs must always remember that the people in front of him have come, often at much expense of money and time, to enjoy themselves in hard work and good music. If they become uncooperative, he is helpless; there are plenty of ways open to the amateur, as to the professional, of sabotaging a rehearsal! If they cease to enjoy themselves, it is probably his fault. If time is wasted, he has a share of responsibility, even if it is some non-musical matter that has gone amiss. Has he done his homework? It can be arduous, especially if orchestral parts have to be numbered and marked. With a chorus, how many different editions are in use? Has he got all the numbers and letters marked in his score?

The following advice to conductors of amateurs will, I hope, be agreed by all, and helpful to some:

(1) Never pretend. If you repeat a passage for the benefit of yourself rather than that of the performers, say so.

(2) Do not be too specific in accusations of bad ensemble or intonation. You probably do not have a Toscanini ear.

(3) Humble yourself by taking a tape recording of your rehearsal, and listen to it for a good time – not just a minute or two. Ask yourself honestly – do you talk too much? Can everything you say be heard by a (slightly deaf) second horn or back-row singer? Above all, is there silence before you say anything, and how many false starts were there, when many people did not know why you had stopped, or where you were starting again? False starts are almost always the fault of the conductor, and are exasperating to anyone who is used to efficient rehearsal. (It is extraordinary how many otherwise competent conductors say, 'Start 1, 2, 3 . . . bars before letter B', instead of 'Before letter B, 1, 2, 3, . . . bars.')

(4) In these days of video recording, it should not be difficult to find a friend to make a video record of your efforts during rehearsal, say from the outside edge of the second fiddles, or the back edge of the chorus. Then ask yourself honestly again, whether you could, out of the corner of your eye and in the middle of a difficult

passage, distinguish the first beat of each bar among your general gyrations? or in a pianissimo passage, where you are trying for a real diminuendo to ppp (i.e. practically inaudible) you really indicate the precise moment at which a given note is to stop, or be changed? I feel that the amateur, however experienced, is entitled to ask this sort of information from his conductor's beat.

(5) Try conducting some of the rehearsal with your left hand in your pocket (except for turning over). What do you normally use it for?

(6) If like most of us, you have only a 'conductor's voice', be reluctant to use it except for a minimum of clear speech.

(7) If you have vocal soloists to rehearse on the day of the concert, try to release them early in the rehearsal. They need to relax before the performance.

I could go on for a long time with comments of this sort, and I expect that every experienced conductor could add his own. I have shown this list to various good friends, and asked whether they agreed; the most unanimous support was for 'don't talk too much'. Another suggestion was 'don't say, "Watch the stick" – say "Listen to everyone else" '. It is the truth, I think, that, in most music, one listens rather than watches, for the best ensemble.

One addition came from a choral singer (not I fancy in complete seriousness) – a remark useful in many circumstances, and I believe attributed to a famous film star, on the eve of his re-marriage to a former wife – 'I know what I've got to do, but the trouble is to make it seem interesting.'

It is tempting for a conductor to think that the secret of a good ensemble and attack is that everyone should follow *exactly* his beat. This in fact is not usually possible, nor indeed desirable (cf. remarks in next section about the leader). The beat from many first-class conductors anticipates the moment at which the sound is expected, by varying times depending on the context. The point is: is the difference consistent for all the performers (remembering such variables as the different speaking times of instruments, and the time taken by sound to travel across a large group of performers)? Some halls are better than others for ensemble, more because everyone can hear everyone else at approximately the same moment (the old Queen's Hall, for example) than because they can see better.

I have already commented on the bad habit of failing to give a visible indication of the precise starting or stopping of a pianissimo note. I once remarked to Archie Camden on the precision with which both bassoons had come in together in the first bar of the second movement of the Brahms Violin Concerto. Boult was conducting, and I personally could see no indication whatever from his beat of this entry. 'It's quite simple,' said Archie; 'we just come in with my foot'.

Every conductor of course builds up a stock of remarks he finds useful to put across a point at rehearsal. My own favourite, with the horns, used to be to remind them of a certain advertisement common at one time on the London Tube staircases, for an intimate article of ladies' wear, which claimed to 'add fullness *confidentially.*'

One final point – a conductor at rehearsal must be articulate. He must have words at hand to express his meaning precisely – if, occasionally, humorously as well, then so much the better! I remember once playing for Kennedy Scott, an admirable conductor on musical grounds, but not easy to follow from a technical point of view. He was dissatisfied with our playing of some Bach; the leader urged him to say precisely what was wrong – were the notes too long or short, crescendos inadequate, more bow, less bow, etc.? All Scott could say was 'No, no, my dear fellow, it must be more staunch . . . staunch . . .' A good word, but not all that was needed in the circumstances.

The Leader

The Leader of an orchestra is obviously an important figure. He is usually expected to be the best violinist present, and often is so; but this is not his essential quality. His value is measured (a) by what the other players think of him: is he a reliable, understanding, friendly person, firm but tactful with careless or recalcitrant players, able to teach on matters of bowing and fingering without offending others who think they know better, able to take an efficient sectional rehearsal? and (b) by his ability to 'split the beat' between conductor and orchestra. Quite apart from major accelerandos and ritardandos, most music is moving either forwards or backwards, a little faster or a little slower (I am talking of hundredths of a second, of course). The lesser players in an orchestra are not usually conscious of this. Even if the beat is precise, in the sense of there being an observable point at which the conductor intends the sound to occur or to alter, that point is ahead (or alternatively behind) the average of the players by a tiny but detectable interval of time. (This is why one has sometimes, in conducting an orchestra, the sensation of trying to control it through a piece of elastic.) In much the same way, turning the steering wheel of a car does not immediately produce a change of direction, as the beginning driver has to learn. Now the good leader, like the skilled driver, manages to keep within this tiny backlash, and his fellows find it easier to follow him exactly (as they think) than to follow the conductor. One effect of a good leader is therefore to make the orchestra much more responsive to those tiny changes of tempo which it is every conductor's ambition to be able to control at will. I have found for this reason some first-class players no good as leaders; either they cannot help playing just as they feel the music should go – in a sense disregarding the conductor – or they anticipate the conductor's intentions so well as to cause confusion among the other players.

Organization

The Organizer(s) of an amateur group (secretary, treasurer, 'fixer', librarian, concert manager, publicity manager, etc.) – several people in a group of any size – have between them a difficult job, in the long run as important as that of the conductor, and less easily recognized as such. There are the over-efficient 'clipboard' types, and the easy-going muddlers, always forgetting, always in arrears. The members of the society must be made to feel that they are individually important at a rehearsal, that their comfort has been considered as far as possible, that information is available and that things are properly planned. There must be provision for gossip and refreshment – the cup of coffee makes all the difference to a long rehearsal, though unpopular with the conductor, who sees the precious minutes ticking away, with so much still to rehearse!

The Librarian has one of the most important jobs. There are much bigger problems today than in a previous generation, with continually rising costs of the purchase, hire, and postage of music. Gone are the days when a pleasant afternoon could be spent at Messrs Novello's comfortable rooms in Wardour Street, looking through their new choral music or being brought scores for inspection by a helpful librarian; or wandering on past Schott and Augener to Goodwin & Tabb in Dean Street, where a selection of unknown works could be borrowed for try-through at that evening's rehearsal for a few shillings. Nowadays, publishers are scattered afar; orders must be placed beforehand, deposits paid, and the cost of hire for even a short period will be measured in pounds for a single vocal score and £50 upwards for an orchestral work of any size – much more, if the work is copyright and a performance is contemplated. Also of course the conductor demands – quite rightly – more expensive and difficult works than he would have done 50 years ago.

Modern publishers seem to have concluded – no doubt from the greater opportunities given by broadcasting and recording – that, as a business proposition, hire and performance fees are more valuable than sales. Orchestral parts of recently published works are not usually on sale; and the purchase cost of vocal scores is often prohibitive to a small Society which wants to try out several works in planning its programme. There were always difficulties for the amateur group in getting certain kinds of music (French and Russian in particular). The old-time publishers must have felt that they had some duty to music as an art rather than just a business, and did not cost their hiring very strictly; 'Messiah' and 'Elijah' must have financed many works in Novello's list which never covered the costs of their production. But nowadays music is big business, and its details are costed as such.

Heavy costs of music must stifle amateur enterprise, and when copying machines are to be found in every office, must encourage clandestine duplication. Fortunately one or two publishers, e.g. Belwyn Mills in U.S.A., are adopting a more enlightened attitude, and sell a wide range of non-copyright music, including many standard vocal/orchestral works, and some operas. Some of these appear to be reproductions of the old Breitkopf & Härtel printings, and though they are not quite so good in appearance and quality, their price has a reasonable relation to the probable costs of production. Belwyn Mills also have intelligent and flexible policies, e.g. in the sale of music already used on hire. There are also small publishers in this country who will meet the needs of choral societies who need comparatively small numbers from the originals (usually out of print), by arrangement with the owners of the copyright. Some publishers however, considering the actual costs of modern reproduction, seem still to make a disproportionate charge for replacing missing copies and the like.

Apart from hire or purchase, the Society's librarian will also have to be familiar with those public libraries (e.g. the Central Music Library in London, and several County Libraries) which have substantial collections of standard music for loan. There are also arrangements, centralized by the N.F.M.S., by which mutual exchanges can take place between societies owning their own libraries. But any such use is likely to involve the amateur librarian in a lot of hard work in packing and sending, and checking and replacing and mending music. Fortunate are those Societies who already possess an appreciable library of the music they need.

The Rehearsal in General

It seems to me that a cardinal principle in an amateur society which gives concerts should be that the rehearsal is what matters, not the concert. If rehearsals are enjoyable, then surely the concert, with its added excitement, will be a success. But several societies tolerate rehearsals which can give no pleasure to anyone concerned.

There are obvious material requirements for a good rehearsal – reasonable space and comfort, a tolerable acoustic, good warmth and light. But deficiencies here may perhaps be accepted – if members feel, for example, that an energetic secretary is doing his best about them. What is fatal to a society is the kind of meeting where no pleasing musical achievement is possible, and it does not appear to matter whether any particular person is there or not. It is then tempting and perhaps justified for player or singer to resolve not to come again, if at all, till the last rehearsal before the concert.

Whose fault will this be? Usually the conductor's, or the fixer's. If there is not going to be, at a particular rehearsal, an attendance good enough to produce a rewarding result, the rehearsal should be cancelled or converted to a sectional meeting where useful work can be done. Orchestras are of course more sensitive than choruses here; if several leading sopranos are to be away, it is still a good opportunity to teach and encourage some of the less confident ones. But an orchestra cannot rehearse a Brahms symphony with profit with only two or three wind players; much better to tell them not to come, and to do useful work with the strings alone. But this demands individual action by the organizer or fixer for each rehearsal, to make sure that no-one is going to waste their time that evening.

Depending of course on the programme, if anyone is needed only for a part of the rehearsal, he must be told exactly when, and for how long. Soloists, semi-chorus, extra percussion, unusual instruments – all must be considered by the conductor or organizer, to make sure that they are not brought to a rehearsal unless they are really needed; and when they are there, they must be given personal attention, not be expected to hang around in uncertainty. Every rehearsal, in fact, will be planned by a competent conductor so that everyone will enjoy it – that is part of his job.

Everyone who has experienced it knows that say four rehearsals just before a concert are more efficient than the same number, spread over four weeks. A great deal can be done in fact in one weekend, starting on Friday night: and this is the plan adopted by some Youth Orchestras and some holiday groups. Perhaps the concentrated meetings suit the young; perhaps also they are more effective in big cities than in smaller communities. The weekly rehearsal may however suit better a society of long standing, where friendly gossip is a valuable part of the whole pleasure, and where traditions have been built up. But a society which is undergoing major changes in policy of other kinds should at least consider what arrangement of rehearsal is likely to suit it best.

The Chorus Rehearsal

A chorus is very different from an orchestra; and very few conductors are equally good with either. The amateur chorus is probably more heterogeneous, both in basic ability and in training and experience, than the orchestral equivalent. It has one big advantage – the upper limit on its performance, assuming that there is time and enthusiasm enough, is musically higher. But this upper limit will need more individual work to reach it, and may not be so obvious when reached.

In general it is fairly evident how good an orchestral player is – the motions of his arms and fingers are very revealing if closely watched, and if he is a wind player he is already a soloist and his playing should be possible to identify. To make any real improvement, say in facility, tone quality, or intonation, he will have to take things seriously, take lessons perhaps, devote regular time to practice; and probably he will not do this. But many choirs will consist largely of untrained singers, and it is not so easy to spot those whose value is negative; it is not sufficient to favour just those whose mouths do open and shut, and whose eyes do appear to be aware of the beat! Good or bad, however, their ability as choral singers can be much improved in a short time under proper direction.

Many of them will never have considered the various components which go into the articulation of a single syllable at the musically right moment; they will have no idea of relaxed and sustained breathing, and are in a sense handicapped by the use of the essential organs of lips, tongue and teeth in quite a different way in normal, probably slipshod, speech. All these matters, from the point of view of choral singing, can be much improved by quite a little intelligent effort. Though of course it would be absurd to think that a properly produced voice could result from a few minutes' exercises at a weekly rehearsal, in the hands of someone who knows what he is talking about (possibly supervised by someone in the choir who is a trained singer), those few minutes can work wonders. This can be seen from the occasional near-perfect performances at Festivals by small village choirs – probably the members are not at all specially picked, but everyone has worked hard individually under good direction.

In aiming at an 'upper limit' of accomplishment, it is the conductor's job to formulate to himself what has to be done to reach it – often a very difficult problem. A little time ago I was listening to the rehearsal of a small and rather good singing group in two very dissimilar works – a Byrd motet, and the Britten 'Hymn to St Cecilia'. I found it very difficult to say just what was needed to bring an already pleasing performance to the high standard of which these singers were certainly capable. Perhaps the Byrd was the more difficult in this respect – to moderate the natural dominance of the sopranos (who had the best voices), to make the altos audible as their phrases went low, to warm the quality of the tenors in the middle of the texture, and to secure real unanimity in lengths of notes and smooth passage from one note to another. The Britten, though looking technically more difficult, I felt to be the easier to rehearse; here slow practice of one or two difficult chords for intonation, and real familiarity with the quick notes and syllables, would soon bring improvement.

(I have often felt that the pitch of short quick notes, particularly of basses low in their compass, is never determinate, even in the singing of good professionals. Fortunately perhaps, the ear-brain of the listener will suggest many things which are not really there, in a physical sense!)

There are of course plenty of books on choir training (refs 13, 14, 21). For a sophisticated choir, Steinitz' description of his methods in learning a difficult modern work is interesting (ref. 41). Anthony Hopkins has written an amusing set of exercises for a chorus, in such points as rhythm, intonation, articulation, etc. in 'Five Studies for Chorus and Piano' (pub. J. M. W. Chester). When a work is very taxing by reason of its high notes (e.g. the 'Missa solemnis'), it should not be necessary for a conductor to ask the sopranos and tenors (the usual victims) to sing the exhausting passages more than once at the right pitch, particularly at the final rehearsal. By learning to sing the passages an octave lower the singers will avoid fatigue – and perhaps learn more about the other parts at the same time.

There are good physiological reasons why articulation on syllables, and the differentiation of vowels, is difficult at the upper part of the soprano range, and in fact it is stated by Halsey (ref. 21) that between the tuning A (440 hz) and the E above it, only two vowels (*ee* and *a*) are distinguishable, and also that above E all vowels sound the same. Halsey is also interesting when he points out that it is probably impossible to avoid singing such phrases as 'world withou ten, damen' or 'O Lorder, open thou our lipser' in the way suggested.

Finance and Policy

It needs little study of the condensed financial statements given in Appendix IV to see that many of the larger amateur societies are in a precarious financial position. They are solvent only by persistent fund-raising, soliciting of grants from N.F.M.S. and other sources, sponsorship, etc. Historically, the wealthy patron has often been the necessary supporter of large-scale music; is this still inevitable in the wealthier society of today?

Working expenses, such as printing, postage, etc. will naturally increase in line with general inflation; but more specific expenses, such as hire of rehearsal rooms and concert venues, and purchase and hire of music, seem sometimes to have risen faster than this. And the revised policies of many education authorities, whereby more realistic charges are being made for evening class fees (which amounts to the disappearance of a subsidy which has been available hitherto), are bearing very hard on some societies.

But above all, the proportion of income that goes in professional fees seems to me to be excessive in some budgets. The policy of many societies, especially the larger and older-established ones, is to put on big programmes with considerable professional help (often a completely professional orchestra), and soloists whose names are familiar through broadcasting and recording. When this is done, the total of professional fees often dwarfs all other expenditure in the budget.

This policy is natural and well-justified for a few big societies with a long tradition of first-class performance – no-one, for example, would suggest diminution of the Bach Choir's annual 'St Matthew' as an authoritative occasion, with no expense spared. And money spent in this way supports a number of excellent professionals, ultimately to the benefit of us all. But I feel that we must consider the basic question – what is an 'amateur' performance for?

Is it primarily to produce the best possible performance, for the benefit of the audience (and critics, perhaps); or is it to produce the maximum of pleasure, in the long run, for that hypothetical individual, the 'average' member of the 'average' musical society? I do not think that these two questions are necessarily equivalent; nor do I think that they are often debated without some noise in the background – that of the sharpening of axes.

At such a debate – should it ever occur – the conductor will feel, naturally enough, that he is a more important conductor if he conducts more important people; and also if (as is often so) he is a professional, that his future career is enhanced by such conducting. The secretary and treasurer will point out that without these well-known names, the hall will be half-empty and there will be a heavy loss; anyway, with an expensive and adventurous programme, the N.F.M.S. (or other sources) may well produce a bigger grant and the society may be no worse off, if indeed at all. And, of course, for all concerned in the organization, it is *much* less trouble to import professionals in the orchestra and to have well-known and experienced soloists than to look locally for talent – perhaps then fewer rehearsals will be necessary, disaster is less likely, the Press is more likely to be interested, and so on.

These are valid and powerful arguments. Nevertheless, I cannot help feeling that sometimes the axe-sharpening is overdone; that the prime purpose of the society is not the maintenance of conductor and professionals, but the production of maximum pleasure (in the widest sense of the term) for all; and that in the long run amateur music (which, let us remember is the most of music) would often benefit from a less ambitious policy, depending less on the big names, in which local talent was looked for and made full use of.

Very good orchestral and singing amateurs exist all over the country, though they may need finding. They are not going to commit themselves to help at concerts unless (a) they are friends with those concerned, (b) they feel sure of a good show, with an inspiring conductor, good conditions (warmth, light, food, acoustics, for example) and efficient rehearsal, (c) they are made to feel that they have a personal share in the success of the show, and are not likely to be relegated to inferior positions by some visitor brought in at the last moment.

Perhaps even good amateur harpists might begin to multiply, if these conditions were maintained!

And there are very good amateur soloists for some occasions – not quite so easy to find, I admit; but there do exist a number of fine singers who (all the above conditions being fulfilled) will sing genuinely as amateurs, if they are sure of real musical satisfaction as the result. I know for example two such tenors whose 'Gerontius' is definitely worth listening to; and if there are two in the limited circle of my acquaintance, there must be a dozen or two in the country as a whole. And good sopranos and baritones are more plentiful than tenors.

In suggesting a greater use of amateurs as soloists, I have already said that I do not have the big and famous societies in mind. But I do feel that a small society, in financial trouble as to its immediate future, or a new society just forming, should consider whether it would not be well advised to abandon the idea of concerts with semi-professional standards, and to see whether concerts could not be as successful, and in the long run audiences better satisfied, with the best local talent, working on a smaller scale. This is probably what would have happened fifty years ago, when money was scarcer, transport more difficult, radio and gramophone less commonplace, and perhaps the amateur performing spirit more vigorous.

The best home cooking may be better for general health and happiness than to live on tinned beans at home and regard a weekly meal at a gourmet restaurant as the main pleasure of eating. Recent comments from a friend, an expert singer, after singing with a number of societies, are perhaps relevant here. 'One wonders whether the members are truly happy to be just the background to the front line of visiting artists, either in the solo or the orchestral roles. If amateur societies collapse from the effects of the current financial scene and the curious upward cycle of aspiration which is affecting all such societies at present, I believe that they will nevertheless begin all over again in some small way, just as before, because there is a driving force to make music which I do not think can ever be killed, either by money troubles or by the effects of mechanical music making and reproduction. I think that growing numbers of such societies almost look forward to this rebirth, small being beautiful, and doing your own thing unaided by someone who is supposed to be better at it than you are, being the most fun of all...'

Old Age

One problem affects all societies sooner or later, and I know of no perfect solution. What is to happen to the old friends, past pillars of the Society, still enjoying themselves and anxious to go on helping, but now falling behind in technique and energy? Tactful suggestion, and some administrative jobs, perhaps; one can hardly adopt the business technique of the golden handshake. But if the Society acquires the reputation of collecting experienced but ageing members, particularly in the key positions, then young people will not be attracted, and the Society must eventually collapse. Probably the only real answer to this problem is a tradition of audition and a re-choice of all performing members each season or so, perhaps a new and ruthless conductor or secretary may be needed; but new brooms are bound to be prickly and so cause distress somewhere.

Conclusion

This chapter has ranged widely over a number of topics; and, in summarizing, I would suggest that if any Society is thinking seriously about its future – perhaps it has had a disconcerting shock of some kind, the retirement of a loved conductor, a disastrous balance sheet, a sudden fall in membership – it should ask itself a number of basic questions. Has it the right officers, particularly the right conductor? Are its rehearsals enjoyable? Are its members paying in subscription, for their weekly rehearsal, for example, as much as they spend on a visit to the pub? And, above all, are young people interested? The youth orchestra and chorus movement (cf. ch. 6) has accustomed large numbers of the best youngsters to good conducting, disciplined rehearsals, and adventurous programmes. Are these youngsters, when they pass the age limit for 'youth', to dissipate their talents and perhaps cease to take part in performing music, just because there is no local music good enough for them? Here I think is the tremendous opportunity for amateur music societies of the future.

Interlude: Partly on Enjoyment

So far I have been describing the activities of a few thousand people who enjoy taking part in choral and orchestral music – friends, or friends of friends, of mine (the word 'friend' must be occurring almost as frequently as 'amateur' in this book!). Could there be a more varied set of pleasures within a common framework – the steady enjoyment of weekly meetings of the Edinburgh chorus, increasing technical accuracy and competence in difficult passages with the Salomon or the Renaissance, the warm welcome on a Sunday afternoon at Oaks Farm, even the laborious telephoning of the 'fixer' for the Chelsea Opera Group as he checks up for the next concert? And I have touched on only a tiny fraction of what goes on all over the country; these pleasures are repeated a thousand times in a thousand contexts.

I am reminded of that delightful book 'England, My England', where the author ends with a daydream on a lazy afternoon, looking out over the green fields of the valley of Winchester. It is curiously misty, and gradually the mist clears to reveal a great procession through the centuries – it is the poets and writers of England, passing by in a laughing, chattering mob. MacDonnell could equally well have made them the amateur musicians of England – just as happy, rather more numerous I would think, and certainly noisier. There would be a host of 10,000 voices at some point, singing the 'Hallelujah' perhaps with Handel conducting; in a quieter corner, Pepys surrounded by a group of lovely ladies, singing and playing with them; somewhere else, a last-night Proms audience with the British Sea Songs under Sir Henry Wood's direction.

For many of us, doing music with one's friends is the happiest of all occupations. But happiness alone is not a complete description of the reasons why we make music; and in the final Chapter (10), I shall try to say at a rather deeper level what music means to me and to many others.

Meanwhile, in the next Chapter (5) I shall talk about Chamber Music, which to many is a sufficient musical world in itself; and then in Chapters 6, 7 and 8, about some topics which may concern the amateur, such as young people's music, holidays with music, finance, and officialdom.

At the end of the book are Appendices, one describing some technical effects of science and technology on instrument construction, and raising the controversial issue of listening tests for quality of tone; and finally, a Bibliography of, I hope, general interest.

5
Chamber Music

I wish I could remember in more detail the first time that I tried to play a string quartet. It was probably at my school, Oundle, where I have recollections of the first movement of Beethoven op. 18 no. 6, very dull at about half-speed, and of a Schumann movement, rather unsuitable for schoolboy players. But I must have spent a fair amount of time on domestic music before I went to Cambridge, as my younger sister still maintains that her pleasure in music was irrevocably spoilt by her being forced to learn the viola clef for my benefit!

The domestic musician does not appear on any lists and gains no publicity; it would be difficult to make an estimate of his numbers, beyond saying that they must be very large indeed; and it would be difficult to over-estimate his importance in the music of the country. A fiddle case, or a readiness to sing, will open doors in many a town or village; London or any large centre is a hive of chamber music; a friend said to me 'anywhere you look in Newcastle or Durham there is active music going on'; this is equally true among my acquaintances in Edinburgh or Bristol.

In the last century, of course, before the advent of gramophone and radio, the standard of amateur performance must often have been deplorable, particularly when it was regarded more as the necessary accomplishment of the polite young lady than as a serious and worthwhile occupation. We remember how Mary Bennett embarrassed her more musical sister Elizabeth by her over-readiness to take her seat at 'the instrument' (an excellent summary of the attitude to music of Jane Austen and other novelists is given by Loesser, ref. 29). But there was competence and devotion as well; a good picture of the amateur in the nineteenth century is given in Shera's book (ref. 39) (almost the only book I know about amateur music as such). I like also an advertisement used by Messrs Novello in 1852 (ref. 24) when they were setting up a branch in U.S.A., which well suggests the domestic scene at the time – 'Some of the best music in England is performed by, say, six families meeting in succession at their parent's houses, all idle or uninterested listeners being excluded; the hour of meeting, 7 o'clock; tea, with its strict concomitants, at nine; and then one hour of lighter music enables each to depart at half-past ten. An evening so spent leaves nothing to regret the next day.' The party which this advertisement had in mind presumably was to sing some of Messrs Novello's multitude of glees and part songs – we wonder what the 'strict concomitants' were – but the general advice is still good, and regular participators in family chamber music will surely have 'nothing to regret the next day'.

That unusual cleric, the Rev. H. R. Haweis (he wrote voluminously on musical biography, Cremona violins, and church bells, and was disliked by Sir George Grove) is also worth a glance for his remarks on the amateur of the period, some of which are still relevant. His book 'Music and Morals' (ref. 22), has paragraphs headed 'People who play the Pianoforte' – 'Concerted Chamber Music' – (this includes out-of-tune flautists and cornet players) – 'The people who Sing' – and 'The Quartet Party', a party of real enthusiasts who are rather good, and play from morning till midnight; they are contrasted with 'The Scratch Quartet', the description of which obviously comes from the heart.

However we define Chamber Music – perhaps as music performable in the home, or as music written basically for one performer per part – most of us will agree that (a) it includes much of the greatest of all music, and (b) much of it was written originally for the amateur, and the composer did not expect or hear performances better than what we should now call of first-class amateur standard, and (c) it is often more appropriate than is larger-scale music to the casual, the impromptu, the humorous – to emphasis on the fun of music, in fact. Though we do not tackle Beethoven's op. 132 without due preparation and reverence, we can pick up a gay madrigal or an early Haydn quartet at any time in any company, and enjoy it without apology or introspection. And in different context, a light-hearted attack on, say, a big symphony with two players at a piano is a good occupation, when a real rehearsal with an orchestra would be a serious undertaking. Hopkins' delightful 'Concerto for two tuning-forks' (the quietest piece I know, taking about 25 seconds to play) is certain to be hilarious in performance.

The spectrum of home music is indeed a vast one. At one end, perhaps, a family group with assorted instruments and voices, some of them complete beginners, their aim being to keep together for a few bars, and find out what fun it all is; at the other, a dedicated quartet or madrigal group, perhaps rehearsing seriously for some private performance. They will be carefully chosen and balanced, of comparable technical skill, having worked together for years. Their music may to them be the high point of the week; they know it almost by heart, and their aim is to bring the quality of their performance just that little bit nearer to the limit set by their technique and musical understanding.

Yet over this spectrum probably Charles Avison's remarks will still apply (from his Preface to Six Sonatas op. 7, for 2 violins, cello and keyboard, 1760):

'This kind of Music is indeed not calculated as much for Public Entertainment, as for private Amusements. It is rather like a Conversation among Friends, where Few are of one Mind, and propose their mutual Sentiments, only to give Variety, and enliven their select Company.'

This 'conversation among friends' has been a major source of the pleasure of my life. In this chapter, I shall try to say something of the friendly background to domestic music; of the variety of possible ensembles; of the habits of 'serious' performers, mainly in string quartets, and of the advice and literature open to them; and finally I shall describe (as I did in an earlier chapter about the larger choral and orchestral groups) some of the organizations which exist for the support of chamber music.

Background

To most amateurs, music is fun first and a deeper enjoyment second. And part of the fun is the friendly meal beforehand or the inter-quartet cup of tea. Fortunate are those ensembles where there is a host(ess) in the background who is not jealous of the music, does not insist on chatty conversation just after some special moment, yet has the tea ready just when it is most needed – a rare art. I am sure that there exist 'quartet widows' just as there are 'golf widows'. Rehearsal certainly reveals character: and it is tempting to imagine standardized types – the dominant leader, the self-satisfied tenor, the extrovert 'cellist, and so forth. But in truth everyone is different, and generalizations may be amusing but are unimportant. All groups however need a leader or master of ceremonies – not the 'first violin' of fiction, but someone who knows what needs to be done, from setting up music stands or chairs, to suggesting that a piece

should be done again or that it is time to do something else, with
firmness and tact. Without him, time will be wasted and maybe
tempers strained.

Remembering the baleful influence of TV and the many other
attractive ways of spending time these days, I cannot think that
many people now know of houses which they can visit, literally
without notice, with a worth-while chance of joining in some music.
As a young man in London, I was fortunate in two such – Edric
Cundell's studio in St John's Wood, where he might well be sitting at
the piano with some students round him saying, 'Come on, let's sing
this ensemble through [probably a bit of 'Figaro'] and then we can
have Brandenburg no. 2, if so-and-so can manage the trumpet part
on his clarinet.' And then the Beavan household in Kilburn, where
the two Beavan brothers, with the flautist Frank Butterworth and
the musical polymath John David Solomon – any instrument, any
voice at a pinch – were usually to be found; and the choice might be
between a rather high-class string quartet and a game of table tennis
or Demon Patience, played with great skill and energy. Mrs Bowen's
book 'Friends and Fiddlers' (ref. 11) conveys very pleasingly
(though with too much sentiment sometimes for the prosaic
Englishman) the atmosphere of just such a home in the U.S.A.,
though in a much more well-to-do and sophisticated setting. In the
winter of 1941 my war-time job took me on my first crossing of the
Atlantic to New York, and one evening landed me in the house of
John Drinker, Mrs Bowen's brother, which was just as I had
imagined – a big music room crowded with an enthusiastic chorus
singing one of the smaller Bach Masses. I was able to describe to the
company the sharp contrast of London's blackout, and to say that
almost at that precise moment my friends in England would be
singing the Mass in B minor!

One trouble with the organization of chamber music at home is
that there is no obvious way of finding out the abilities of a stranger
or visitor beforehand; and a bad mistake can wreck the evening for
everyone. That occasionally amusing book 'The Well-Tempered
String Quartet' (ref. 8) suggests that gaps in an incomplete ensemble
can be filled by advertising; and at one time 'The Musical Times'
used to carry an 'Amateur's Exchange' column for this purpose. I do
not know how far public advertisements can be successful, and there
may have been awkward evenings when some obviously unsuitable
stranger turned up. Nevertheless, when something happens – there
is a mistake over a message, or the 'cellist is suddenly ill – it is

tantalizing to reflect that, in a large city at any rate, there are probably several suitable substitutes who would be delighted to come at short notice – but how to find them? In the computer world of the future, we shall all no doubt be categorized, not only as to our technique and musical understanding, but also for personal charm and likelihood of being free on Tuesday evenings; resort to the 'Dial-a-cellist' service will then no doubt provide a speedy replacement. (The honest computer will presumably also list defects, not purely musical ones – such as unreliability in turning up, stamping the rhythm with the feet or the habit of a loud sniff on the first beat of the bar.)

One serious attempt at providing information among amateurs is made by the U.S.A. organization, 'Amateur Chamber Music Players', well known to many in England. The A.C.M.P. is a remarkable body which has grown up, in some 35 years, from a small group of friends into a widespread movement, now with 6000 members, scattered far beyond the U.S.A.; it is essentially a manifestation of the personal abilities and devotion of a lady, Helen Rice, of immense energy and charm, to whom all chamber music players were friends. Alas, she died in 1979; but the organization which is her best memorial carries on with vigour. It publishes a Directory with the names and addresses of its members, many of whom undertake to try to fix up chamber music for anyone visiting a strange town. (A somewhat similar list is now being started in Great Britain under the auspices of the Rural Music Schools Association). The A.C.M.P. issues to its members a self-assessment form, after a pattern which I suggested to Helen Rice many years ago, originally for string players; but now extended to cover other instruments, and also singers (further detail is given in Appendix III). It has also produced a 'List of Recommended Chamber Music' which contains details of many unfamiliar works.

TYPES OF ENSEMBLE

Trio-Sonata

The trio-sonata (for two treble and one bass instruments, with a keyboard background) is probably the most suitable form of chamber music for the beginner or for a team of limited ability (recorder and viol ensembles, in which many make their first acquaintance with ensemble playing, are mentioned later). Three independent parts give satisfactory counterpoint and harmony; though the bottom line should in general be played by a gamba or cello, with harpsichord backing, at need a pianist will serve, if he is musical and discreet enough to avoid the thick chords and unnecessary ornaments which spoil many older editions. A bassoon can play with him; the two upper parts will often suit woodwind instead of strings; the literature is extensive. The beginning will find much that he can tackle in trio-sonatas, and expert players can fully exercise their musicianship and skill, within the neat framework of such music.

Madrigal

The madrigal, at its best perhaps when in five parts, is a very satisfactory form for music at home, although it is almost as difficult to find a well-matched voice team as to find equal players for a string quartet. Perhaps there is no real tenor available; or one of the singers has a large voice with a wobble which will not blend with the rest; or one is such a poor reader as to hold up everyone else. But with a good team there is a great fund of pleasure in those blue books of the Fellowes edition (and, of course, in the Italians), though perhaps not the lifetime's occupation which some find in the string quartet literature.

Less organization perhaps is needed for the domestic madrigal than for any other form of chamber music; no instrument, a room, the music, and maybe a cup of tea in the middle. The 'tea' of course can be improved on; one small group containing several of my friends, meeting once a month in each other's houses, for music from Renaissance to 20th-century, calls itself the 'Gloo' club – an elision of 'Kew Glee Club', which is rather hard to say after a sufficiency of wine!

String Quartet

The string quartet (with its near relations, the string trio, quintet, etc.) is to its devotees the most satisfactory form of chamber music. I will return to it when I have mentioned some other forms of ensemble.

Piano Repertory

String players are sometimes a little reluctant to include a pianist in their evening's music; partly because, though there are many magnificent piano trios, quartets and quintets, there is not so much choice and variety as among the purely string pieces; partly because good intonation always seems, if not more difficult, at least somehow different; but mainly I think because even the best of amateur pianists find it difficult to efface themselves when effacement is needed, and to support rather than to dominate the ensemble. They have so many more notes to play than the strings that only a near-professional technique can prevent this from becoming obvious. A really first-class player is of course a joy; the best pianist with whom I ever had the privilege of playing was Eric Harrison; with him at the keyboard, all the string players felt that they had never played so well in their life before.

Works with Wind

An experienced string quartet will obviously want to add wind players sometimes to their ensemble, for such works as the Mozart and Brahms Clarinet Quintets, and the Schubert Octet. Caution is needed! Though nowadays there are some outstanding amateur players around, there are also many who may be facile players of their instrument, but who do not realize how hard it is for a wind player to play inconspicuously for many bars at a time, to accompany instead of to play solo, and to listen to everyone else, the first virtue of the good ensemble player. Even with good players, if several in the team do not know a work such as the Schubert Octet really well, a play-through is likely to be noisy and insensitive, everyone playing up to the clarinet or horn in average loudness, rather than down to the first fiddle as would normally happen in a good string team. On such an occasion there is perhaps a case for inviting an outside 'conductor' with a score, with authority to insist on a few real pianissimos!

Wind Alone

The really first-class works for wind and strings are unfortunately few; and the keen wind player who does not want to play exclusively in orchestras has to extend his repertoire in works for wind alone. There are modern (and often very difficult) compositions from trios upwards, and flourishing groups which play them. There is a variety of Mozart pieces for many combinations, including the famous Divertimento for 13 wind – hardly a piece for a small bed-sitter, but magnificent music, and memorable to me as the last piece (in recent years) in which I was allowed to fill a gap as a clarinettist! There is serious music for ensemble of a few brass instruments; and the wind octet (two oboes, two clarinets, two bassons and two horns) is an accepted form with many good players, and for that matter with those of less accomplishment. My friend Elizabeth Foster, a good amateur as soprano or percussionist, gave me an amusing description of the 'Broken Reed Ensemble' which she organizes, 'This was founded some years ago when some of us got together and decided that if four string players could scrape painfully away with every sign of enjoyment, apparently regardless of the sounds produced, we could surely do the same with wind instruments. . . . Plenty of music does exist for various combinations of wind if you take the trouble to dig it out. Now and again we could persuade "real" players to join us and play octets. I think it was Geoffrey Hartley who said that he always enjoyed playing in a "Broken Reed" session because of the backchat between movements and when we broke down.' (Some account of Geoffrey's more serious wind music is given later on.)

Early Music

I believe that modern scholarship does not quite endorse the conventional picture of an Elizabethan society in which any cultivated person could take hand or voice in chamber music on request. Whatever was the reality, there is no doubt that a rich literature collected round voice, lute, recorder, viols, and so forth, and many amateurs today take a keen pleasure in music of this period. There are active societies for recorder and viol playing, many teachers and professional recitals, and a keen market in instruments. Whenever I have placed a sextet by Byrd or a quartet by Jenkins, say, before a good team, but one used only to 19th-century music, it is remarkable how badly they get on to start with, though the notes may be technically quite easy. When performed as it should be, some of this music is of the highest chamber music quality.

THE STRING QUARTET IN PARTICULAR

I shall not I think offend my wind-blowing friends if I say that the finest chamber music that exists has been written mainly for the string quartet, and in consequence the most devoted and experienced amateur is usually a quartet player.

Most of the great composers have written fine quartets, and to get to know their output really well can be the main musical satisfaction of an amateur's life. Many good players, if forced to a choice between quartet music and orchestral playing (e.g. through lack of time or energy for both) would choose the former. By the time that the best of the repertoire – the 10 Mozart, some 30 Haydn, 17 Beethoven, three Schubert, three Brahms, a Dvořák or two, Ravel and Debussy, let us say – have become thoroughly familiar, each will have been played dozens of times, difficult passages will have been individually studied, probably a few private performances will have been given; in the process, many thousands of happy hours will have been spent, and dozens of friendships made – for it is not possible to play music with others for any length of time with real satisfaction, unless there is personal affection as well as musical agreement.

A devoted player of the kind I am thinking of will, of course, be spending a great deal of time and energy on his music – not probably a great deal of his money (though he may hanker after some expensive instrument, may sometimes arrange for professional coaching, and may attend summer schools and master classes). He may become fussy and particular as to whom he plays with; people vary very much in this respect. His path may not be a smooth one, his ambition (perhaps to play a Bartók quartet well enough for some competent critic to consider it worth listening to) may be frustrated by the difficulty of finding three others who will work as hard as he; perhaps he marries a wife who will not allow so much time to be given up to music; perhaps he hears some outstanding performance, so much beyond what he could ever do, that he stops playing, locks up his instrument, and takes up bridge or cabinet-making. Maybe it is a mistake to take too seriously what cannot be a completely full-time devotion. Anyway, let us wish him well!

At all levels of skill and experience, there is of course plenty of advice in books. Page's 'Playing String Quartets' (ref. 32) is one of the best, full of sensible and practical advice on the choice of works and how to rehearse them. Page is encouraging to the disappointed perfectionist – 'the greater the music, the easier it is to give a satisfying if not an impeccable performance. Great music shines through technical imperfections as lesser works do not. ... Many players have more understanding than they have technique, and would be quite mistaken to assume, through diffidence, that the greatest quartets are not for them.'

Gertler also gives good advice (ref. 17). He points out that it is harder even for a first-class player to play really well something like Beethoven op. 59 no. 2, 2nd movement, where difficult semiquavers have to fit in with everyone else, than to dash off a showy piece on one's own, e.g. a Paganini Moto perpetuo. For improvement of intonation, he recommends slow practice of passages, two players at a time; and also the devising of exercises for the quartet together, to get agreement on the precise type of crescendo or sforzando. Talking of the sociability necessary for a stable quartet, he says that Huberman (though he enjoyed quartet playing very much) when asked why he had never formed a quartet, replied 'Que voulez-vous? Je n'ai pas encore eu la chance de trouver trois gentlemen!'

Though most good players have at some time practiced the equivalent of Ševčik, i.e. technical exercises designed to isolate one particular difficulty, and to concentrate the practice in this one direction for the moment, e.g. intonation, accuracy of rhythm, velocity, bow control, etc. – yet I know of no amateur team, among the several serious ones of my acquaintance, who regularly design or use such exercises as a quartet. I would have thought that the results of five minutes' work, at the beginning of each session, would have been as excellent as the corresponding discipline with a small choral group.

To learn a work thoroughly, it is good to play it with inferior players, when you may find yourself responsible for saying exactly what has gone wrong, which needs good listening; it is also good to play with people much better than yourself so that your own musical and technical limitations become apparent. It is also surprisingly difficult, and most educative, even when sitting outside a team and following with the score, to say *exactly* why a given passage is inferior to the same passage as played in a first-class performance.

Anyone who wants to test his knowledge of quartets can try the game called 'Beetholocation' (or Mozart- or Haydn-location, rather simpler). The quartet sits with the complete volume of (17) quartets on their desks. The second violin, who must be a player of impeccable rhythm and tempo, turns aside, so that the others cannot see his copy; and starts anywhere he likes (not necessarily at the beginning of a movement) and goes on playing, regardless, until the others have joined in. It is often a long time before everyone, even with some mutual consultation, has joined in to complete the movement!

ORGANIZED CHAMBER MUSIC

The music I have been talking about so far is not 'organized' in the usual sense; it does not usually aim at performance as such, it needs no particular facilities other than a room and a telephone. But there are some who need more than this – perhaps stimulus from others of like interests, bigger rooms than their own, a library of chamber music, a friendly audience from time to time.

The establishment of Music Centres in some places helps to meet these needs. But nowadays to start a regular 'club' of the old-fashioned kind, for a select few perhaps, in comfortable rooms always available for music, gossip and refreshment, in a central position in a big city, is financially out of the question (though a chance for a musical millionaire, no doubt). There are still one or two groups, perhaps established in more spacious days, which offer something of these favourable circumstances for chamber music. The Oxford and Cambridge Musical Club, for example, before the War was a proper residential Club, but now has no premises of its own: it carries on successfully with regular concerts at which members play and sing to each other. The Kingston and District Chamber Music Society runs similar concerts. The Music Clubs of Bristol and of Edinburgh have their own premises still. On a rather different basis is the Madrigal Society in London, with a history going back to 1741. I will give a little more detail about these and some other groups in the remainder of this chapter, ending with some interesting comments from Roger Wildman in Shetland on the music which he meets there.

Oxford and Cambridge Musical Club

The Oxford and Cambridge Musical Club started auspiciously in 1899, in what had been Sir Joshua Reynolds' house in Leicester Square; it moved to a beautiful Georgian house in Bedford Square which it leased from the British Museum, and which was its home till

1940. Its original membership was distinguished, with Joachim as its first President, and such names as Vaughan Williams, Walford Davies, Henry Hadow and A. C. Mackenzie on its original list. It was a real 'club' in the old style, with half a dozen rooms for the use of members, bedrooms available, the club's considerable chamber music library and two grand pianos to hand, a resident caretaker; one could drop in at any time for congenial conversation, friendly – or occasionally eccentric – company, and music. There were usually weekly meetings at which members could perform to each other; a comfortable all-male society with evening dress for concerts and special occasions, and an occasional 'Ladies' Night'. There were close links with the Music Clubs at Oxford and Cambridge Universities, and a regular interchange of concerts. To give an idea of values in this period, the total in 1930 for rent, rates, etc. was £372 p.a. (though shortly to be raised); resident members paid about £70 p.a. for an unfurnished room, or 5/6d for a night. Against some opposition, women were admitted as members in 1938.

Odd periods of financial difficulty in the 1920s and 30s were overcome, probably with help from individual members. But in 1940 it was apparent that a residential Club with its own comfortable quarters was no longer financially possible.

In the difficult post-war period, the Club was in abeyance, and might easily have been wound up but for the keenness of a few members who were determined that it still had a future, even though it now had no home for its music or instruments, and no meeting place for conversation or concerts. (I have to confess that when my own opinion was canvassed about the future of the Club, my response was a negative one.)

Quoting by permission from the History of the Club (ref. 42) written for its 80th anniversary in 1978:

'The O&C Musical Club could have been transformed into a concert society competing with the many others that have sprung up in London and the provinces since the War, to provide a platform for professional and other executants, and to attract audiences sufficient to defray costs. At times this transition could have been made with relative ease, but it never was. The Club maintained, and retains today, its original character as a member's club, in which members (predominantly amateurs) prepare and perform the music, and members and their friends provide the audience. The story of the years from 1948 to 1978 is one of the gradual replacement of the social stability of an institutional Club by a new kind of stability, relying on the pull of a high level of practical participation by members.'

In the fifties sporadic concerts were organized at a number of places; some were at a member's house in Hampstead, when it was hoped that anyone turning up could be fitted into the music somewhere! And during this difficult period, some quite large and ambitious parties were held, including concert versions of several Mozart operas with orchestra. But in 1959 a fairly regular arrangement was made with University College for the use of one of their common-rooms for the Club's concerts every fortnight, and since then the pattern has become fairly stable. Surprisingly, in view of the number of small orchestras in London all competing for players, small orchestral items, or complete orchestral programmes, have become quite popular; 'Gala' concerts with some special kind of programme, often involving contacts with the Oxford or Cambridge University clubs, occur fairly frequently. Originality has been shown by the organizers of individual programmes in suggesting a special interest, e.g. compositions by members of the Club, and serenade-type programmes in unusual and pleasant surroundings. The general principles are that non-members of the Club should not perform at concerts unless there is special reason; and that the opportunity of performing should be spread as widely as possible.

Kingston and District Chamber Music Society

Several of my friends play regularly with this Society, and owe to it many of their musical contacts. I quote from the account given me by Theo Wyatt, recent chairman of the Society. 'Founded in 1954; a shaky start, but now rudely healthy! 144 members (1982) of whom 10 are non-players, 12 are singers, and 30 pianists. There is a monthly concert (non-members perform only by special dispensation). Regular features are a summer outing – a day of chamber music, held in recent years at Southlands College, requiring a feat of organization so that the 40 or 50 participants can be fitted into different but viable groups for each of the four sessions; an annual children's concert, where the performers are children of the members; an annual workshop or coaching session at the Menuhin School; a members' list with names, addresses, telephone numbers and instruments; an introduction service – certain members have the specific task of finding suitable musical partners for new members on request.

'Each Committee member organizes one or more of the monthly concerts. He has a general duty to ensure that as many members as possible are given an opportunity to perform. He will therefore gently discourage those who have already performed once or twice that season. Subject to that consideration he may either wait for offers from members, or, more rarely, establish a theme for his concert and invite particular contributions from particular members. Audiences are rarely less than 60 and in one or two cases have been over 100.

'Meetings are held in a local church hall, but this is not very good acoustically, and a better site is being looked for; there are also difficulties with pianos. Rehearsals are usually in private houses; there is no financial help from outside, and a small annual subscription covers miscellaneous expenses.

'The great majority of members live within five miles of Kingston. For them the Society provides a ready-made entree into the large circle of like-minded amateurs, and, through regular performance opportunity, an incentive to improvement. These are so valuable that it is a constant source of wonder to those connected with the Society that similar groups do not spring up in every centre of population.'

The Madrigal Society

The great majority of amateur madrigal singing hardly needs 'organization' – the groups are formed easily, and need not last for long. But as long ago as 1741 a small group of London workmen met together to sing madrigals; and their successors still do so to this day – this is thought to be the oldest amateur music group in the country. There is a good account of its history in the New Grove; somewhere round 1820 the members began to meet for dinner, to be followed by singing; and it looks as if the social level began to rise. The connection of the Madrigal Society with the present book is that its current Secretary is Keith Maries, well known in London as a very good horn player; his mother was also one of the first of the 'singing ladies' brought in to sing the upper parts; and my daughter-in-law and her sister are in the same distinguished band at the moment. (There is a more detailed history up to 1955 by Craufurd.)

The Society meets every month in the winter, nowadays at the Tallow Chandler's Hall; there are 40 members. After a good dinner, the 'singing ladies' are admitted, and madrigals are sung according to a programme chosen and conducted by the Musical Director; healths are drunk, and there are several pleasant ceremonials. Recruitment is by personal recommendation; there is usually a waiting list. The Society possesses a large and historic collection of music, and sings from traditional bound volumes which must have been handled by generations of distinguished musicians – many such have been members of the Society, and E. H. Fellowes was Musical Director for many years. On the programmes it is customary to print the number of times that each of the chosen madrigals has been sung by the Society since 1900 – on a programme which I saw for February 1984, Pearsall's 'Take Heart' had scored 95 appearances, and Weelkes' 'The Period of Cosmography' 57. Everything is very pleasant and sociable, and the standard of singing is good.

Quoting from Craufurd's short History, already mentioned, 'The Society is a survival of the eighteenth century, which in the course of time has undergone changes, but remains essentially the same. It is a social meeting place, where musicians, whether professional or amateur, when so inclined, can sing madrigals for their own pleasure, without thought of an audience. May it continue to flourish.'

The Accrington Clef Club

In 1903 in Accrington, Lancashire (a medium-sized cotton spinning town), a music club was born, thought by its present members to be unique. The active spirit was a prominent local musician, George Oldham, who together with 15 other enthusiasts formed an exclusively male club for the enjoyment of music under ideal conditions. The rules were few and simple, but apparently well conceived, for they have needed little amendment during the club's long life, and it is still a thriving organization, quietly fulfilling the hopes and aspirations of the original 16 founders. These men, some of them highly accomplished executants, soon attracted others with similar interests, but remained as a core or club within the club. When they lost one of their number by death or removal from the distrct, he was replaced, so that the club is still governed by sixteen so-called 'founders'.

Membership of the Accrington Clef Club is restricted to one hundred (there is usually a waiting list), and the eight musical evenings held during the winter months take place in the Accrington Mechanics Institute, where the club has the use of a fine room which houses the club's own two grand pianos. The musical items are contributed by members at the invitation of the Programme Committee, and range widely over the chamber music repertory of instrumental and vocal music. Occasionally professional friends are invited to perform, but mainly the platform is taken by the Club's own amateur talent.

The atmosphere is always relaxed and informal, so that aspiring performers are set at their ease. The concerts generally provide for two hours of actual music making, with a half hour interval for refreshments. Within the Club's ranks there is a regular string quartet which combines with the pianists and other instrumentalists as required. The proceedings are never reported in the press, but a careful record is kept of all the works played or sung. Over the whole period of its existence, namely 1903 to the present date, this is, of course, a considerable list.

(The above description is in the words of Dr Jolly, who became a 'founder' in 1936 and took the chair at the 500th meeting of the Club in 1973.)

Bristol Music Club

There is a lot of amateur music in Bristol – choruses and orchestras of different complexions, much chamber music, and an active University stimulus. The Bristol Music Club is particularly interesting because it is a chamber music and orchestral Club, operating in its own premises. It was founded in 1937 by the amalgamation of two clubs (one for women, one for men); the constitution provides for a share-holding Company which maintains the premises and furniture for the Club rehearsals and concerts. There is a large basement, old and somewhat expensive to retain in repair, which will seat an audience of 120, with two grand pianos; also a smaller room, a kitchen, and a bar. There are fortnightly rehearsals for the Club's orchestra, all players in which must be members of the Club; and chamber concerts, usually given by members of the Club, on alternate weeks. The rooms are open for the use of members for most of the week; some income is from their hire to other organizations.

They can be reserved for practice by members of the Club. With economical administration, and few outgoing expenses, the membership subscription is able to keep things in balance.

Occasional Wind Players

This is a London-based group of amateur wind players of unusual ability and permanence. Geoffrey Hartley (referred to elsewhere in this book) in 1948 joined with Arthur Campbell – scientist and teacher, excellent horn player and chamber pianist, with a wide knowledge of all kinds of music – to play music at an Open Afternoon at the London University Observatory at Mill Hill; this was arranged by Ann Robinson, clarinet player, who was working at the Observatory. The works performed – round the big telescope – were the Mozart wind-octet Serenades in C minor and E flat. The players enjoyed the occasion and decided to go on playing together. They have continued to do so, with many changes of players, till the present day, and have given, as amateurs, 270 concerts, at schools, colleges, music clubs, churches, garden parties, weddings, government establishments, a prison, and in fact anywhere where people are sufficiently interested to want to hear them, in return for a meal and travelling expenses. All concerts are arranged by invitation, through members of the Players; there is no advertising.

The octet (two each of oboe, clarinet, bassoon and horn) is the basic constitution of the group, with a flautist on occasion to make a nonet, and additional players for such works as the Mozart Serenade for 13 wind, and the Strauss for 16. Programmes average an hour and a quarter of playing time, and may include some works for a smaller group (to give the oboes a rest, for example). Many people asked to plan programmes for such a group would think perhaps first of one or two favourite pieces by Mozart and then fall back on a mass of material by indifferent composers. Not so the O.W.P., who have two very competent and prolific arrangers in their midst, and have had some dozen works specially composed for them by outside composers, and 30 or more by Geoffrey Hartley. So the programmes, which are full of variety, will contain, besides these original compositions, arrangements varying widely from Bach and Brahms to Rossini and Strauss, sometimes with a lighter touch in short pieces for unusual combinations, Geoffrey and others being versatile performers and having available a collection of many wind instruments: occasional works for serpent, for example, might appear!

A fully detailed list has been kept of performers and works at each concert, and it makes interesting reading for anyone like myself who knows many of the players concerned. Geoffrey has played in 268 out of the 270 concerts (up to 1982), and his fellow-arranger, Arthur Campbell, in 252. There are three others who score 138 or more; five others above 50; so that the team as a whole has been very stable. The list of 43 oboes, 28 clarinets, 25 bassoons and 26 horns who have at one time or another played with the O.W.P. seems to include most well-known amateurs in the London area, and several who have gone on to professional distinction.

Edinburgh Society of Musicians

This is another of the few societies which has its own premises – an attractive centrally-placed music room with two grand pianos, a large library, smaller rooms and a bar, very suitable for musical and social purposes. But this is not an unmixed blessing, as the heavy expenses of a permanent establishment overshadow the Society's balance sheet and make it necessary to supplement income continuously by outside letting of its rooms.

The Society is of long standing, having been founded in 1887 'to cultivate the art and practice of music in Edinburgh and to promote social intercourse among musicians and those interested in music.' Though many distinguished professionals have appeared as members or performers, the membership has been predominantly amateur. The rooms are open on Saturday evenings through most of the year, and weekly concerts are arranged; many ensembles, professional and amateur, regard the society as a good forum for public appearance, and offer their services for concerts. Besides these, there will in the average month's programmes be one with members only as performers, and one devoted to fund-raising.

For much of its history, the Society has been exclusively male (though a parallel Women's Club was in operation); in the last few years, women have been admitted as members. The list of distinguished members and performers is impressive; and the Society presents annually a Gold Medal for some vocal classes at the Edinburgh Competitive Musical Festival and has a Benevolent Fund which can assist professional musicians in need. A recent successful application for charitable status, and the sale to the National Museum of Scotland of various memorabilia, manuscripts, etc. has much improved the financial future of the Society.

Edinburgh Music Club

This club was founded about six years ago by a group of amateur musicians who felt that there should be occasions when they could meet informally and play to each other at regular intervals. Meetings now occur each month, and consist of music played by members of the Club, organized and arranged from one meeting to the next. Membership is open to all, there being no criteria for membership except a love of music; even non-performing members are welcome. The general aims and type of organization are rather like those of the Oxford & Cambridge Musical Club (q.v.); in fact, two of the founding members had been members of this Club. The excellent facilities of the Edinburgh Society of Musicians (q.v.) are used for the concerts; programmes are circulated in advance to the members, and an attempt is made to involve as many members as possible in music-making during the course of the year. Current membership stands between 50 and 60.

The 'member' concerts usually include solo singing, string quartets, piano and wind band items. On two evenings a year music making is organized on a slightly larger basis; small chamber orchestra works, for example, might be rehearsed and then performed during the course of the evening.

One of the chief functions and aims of the Club is to offer a group and a place where musically-minded people can meet and chat; in particular, an effort is made to help newcomers to Edinburgh to meet others and to arrange music for themselves. In recent years the Club has been invited to give concerts to other local music clubs; and this is a way, the Committee feel, to enable some of the best of Edinburgh amateur music-making to be heard by a slightly wider audience.

Efforts are made to celebrate important music anniversaries; the music of William Walton was featured in 1982, and at a recent Stravinsky concert, besides the Sonata for Two Pianos (1943–44) and the Shakespeare Songs (1953) for voice, flute, clarinet and viola, there were two performances of the Septet (1952–53).

The financial side of the Club is at present very simple. The major expense is the monthly hire of the rooms; administration (mainly postage) is kept at a minimum, and the members' subscription is adjusted to cover the total expenditure.

Music in Shetland

Roger Wildman – his address is 'Quartets, Gulberwick, Shetland' – sent me an interesting account of music in his remote habitat.

'There was no secondary education here (Lerwick) until 1868, but a Moravian teacher, John Glass, organized a performance of "Elijah" in 1846, the same year as the first performance in England at Birmingham! In the early 20th century, "Messiah" and some G & S operas were both done each year with a string band. A Lerwick orchestra, formed about this time, got an annual grant of £25 from a local trust fund; but in 1926 it was disbanded after arguments as to whether to practice just for fun, or for concerts. It was re-formed in 1936.

'In World War II the population here doubled, with service men. Some RAF professional musicians played in and conducted the orchestra. In the 1960s, an Education Committee appointed the first full-time strings teacher; there was also a revival of traditional fiddle playing, boosted by T.V. interest.

'There is now a small local madrigal group, "Capella". Though there had been some organized informal singing before this, in 1978 a former Assistant Professor from the R.A.M. formed this concert-oriented group. It performs unaccompanied Renaissance/part-song literature which would not be attempted by the local Choral Society. There are 8 singers (including the Director); rehearsals are at people's homes, monthly but twice weekly before a concert, which is annual, with extra church and radio performances; all proceeds go to charity. All expenses are shared; new members are chosen by personal assessment and canvassing. There is a benevolent dictatorship, but vocal members' ideas are incorporated, and some tasks are shared.

'The initial attraction was that of entering an elite with an artistic mission, since unaccompanied singing is rarely heard up here. Added to this was a tradition of good fun and philosophy, frank gossip after singing, escape from domestic chores by women and from work monotony by men. Problems sometimes arising are – occasional absenteeism; small differences in taste; and some find sight-reading difficult.'

Roger then produces what he calls 'armchair sociology' as follows: 'Amateur music, excluding working class and (mainly male) brass bands, seems to me to serve as a major English middle-class status symbol. I'm an enthusiast for this and many other bourgeois features, and blame their absence here (Orkney, more fertile, is more bourgeois) for some of my problems in organizing quartets and madrigals. Independent schools, investment (= 'deferred gratification'), parental interest in education, identification with independent people, and ambition to progress from local dialect through national to international culture are characteristically English middle-class virtues. Amateur music offers good company, nostalgia (in a good sense like a classic serial), therapy (group), order, ritual, non-verbal communications – a refuge from the categories of science, responsibilities of medicine, strain of teaching, stress of business, triviality of domestic duty. I'm amazed that everyone doesn't play and sing.'

I should like to close this chapter on Chamber Music by a quotation from a distinguished Harvard Professor, who has played his (amateur) viola in fifty countries, to which his professional work has taken him. He is writing about the Amateur Chamber Music Players, already mentioned in this chapter; but what he says has a wider application:

'To describe the A.C.M.P. as an "organization" is to make an implicit criticism of all other organizations . . . it has procedures that put others to shame. A.C.M.P. does not merely approve the minutes of its last meeting, but savors the minutes of every meeting; it does not merely discuss resolutions, but achieves them for each item on its agenda and for each cadence; it does not pass motions, but performs movements; its leadership does not have to be elected, but is a function of the requirements of each situation; membership in it comes not by application, but by practice; it does not seek consensus, but harmony. When you add that the only politics that have to be played in order to achieve priority is between two fiddlers who can compromise by exchanging seats, the reproach to other organizations appears all the greater.'

6
Youth and the Future

In ten years time, if anyone reads this book as far as this, he may well think it very out of date. For the incoming tide which is invading the shores of amateur music, refreshing its rock pools, obliterating some of the mud flats and ancient landmarks, is surely that of the young player and singer.

The Register of the National Federation of Music Societies lists perhaps 800 choral and orchestral societies, say 60,000 active members. Many of these will be vigorous societies, with inspiring conductors, enthusiastic organizers, attractive musical programmes, and no recruitment difficulties. But just as there is (as I have already said) an inescapable problem with the ageing performer, so also there is with the ageing society as a whole. A society is a potentially unstable organism. The loss of one or two key members may encourage others to leave the group and perhaps form other loyalties; if the standard of music and of enthusiasm falls below a certain level, decay is rapid, and there is nothing left but a group of indifferent performers, perhaps lamenting past glories, and condemned to incomplete and uninspiring rehearsals and concerts which can hardly attract their friends. Fortunately, some societies manage to avoid this fate, and to settle into a pleasant equilibrium, where there is still room somewhere for the old friends, but also newcomers find something to attract them, including the chance to take a leading part in the future music of the Society.

But, of course, for the young it is often, and rightly, more attractive, to join a group designed particularly for them. And in recent years, the development of Youth Orchestras and Youth Choirs has been rapid. The Register of the National Association of Youth Orchestras lists some 250 orchestras, say 15,000 young people; many have been established within the last 15 years; many are run through the local education authority, but some are independent and organized by the members themselves, perhaps even with no adults on the committee. Many of the players of course will be at comparatively low grades in the music examination system; but many will be of quite a high standard, potential entrants to the Colleges and the profession, should they decide on a career in music. Besides these orchestras of the symphony orchestra pattern, there are very numerous jazz and brass bands, distinction in which will sometimes lead to money and admiration at an early age. And some of these orchestras, particularly those called 'County' or 'National', are of amazing technical standard; they exceed in finish and performance any normal amateur group, they are full of enthusiasts who are proud of what they do, they are accustomed to hard work and professional discipline at rehearsals, they are fully able to sustain a concert tour abroad with credit – such tours being a normal part of their programme. The development of youth choirs has not been so spectacular, but it is on the way. There are County Youth Choirs of high standard, and a British Youth Choir which aims at really expert singing. A new organization, the British Federation of Youth Choirs, has just been formed to provide help and stimulus where it is needed.

Altogether it seems to me probable that, looking ahead ten years, the main amateur music making will be as much with the young as with the old. I am in personal touch with only a tiny fraction of what is going on, but I have talked to several of the conductors and teachers who are concerned, and to those who come to the 'Junior Orchestra Camp' usually held in the Spring at Pigotts, under Music Camp auspices, and I give here a few examples.

Kent is a good county for the young musician. There is a wide range of standard; the Maidstone Youth Music Society is one of several under the wing of the Maidstone Youth Club, and children join from various schools around; perhaps 150 in all, with 50 in the orchestra, 50 in a wind band, and 50 in a junior group. Music grades from 4 to 6 would be expected from newcomers; there are rehearsals each week, quite a number of concerts to audiences of parents and friends, and an age range from 12 to 19. Few of these children will go on to a professional training; but at a higher level of talent is the Kent County Youth Orchestra. This meets for three separate weeks each year, during the holidays; the summer meeting is largely an audition course for newcomers, junior (under 18) and senior (under 21). Sectional and full rehearsals are intensive, with many teachers and coaches in evidence; 4 or 5 sessions a day, two concerts rehearsed for at the end of each week; a Festival Hall concert each year, and tours abroad (the Orchestra was invited to represent Britain at the Rome Festival in 1983). The courses are residential, the County paying half the cost, so that parents have to provide about £45 for each course. Many of the children concerned are aiming at a professional career, and about 50 have succeeded in this during the lifetime of the Orchestra. Kent has also two brass bands and two bands for jazz and lighter music.

There are similar opportunities for young players in Bedford. Here are four graded youth orchestras, four bands and a junior string orchestra. The senior orchestras have three courses of about a week each; these are non-residential for the most part, but a widespread bussing scheme is in operation for most rehearsals. Each course ends with one or two concerts; some involve travel – the Edinburgh Festival, Paris and Cyprus recently. Several of the children expect to go to one of the music colleges for professional training.

The Stoneleigh Youth Orchestra has a longer history than some, having been founded in 1944 as an offshoot of an adult orchestra in Surrey. Its present conductor, Adrian Brown (also a well-known conductor at Music Camp) has been with it since 1973, and it has grown into a full-sized symphony orchestra of some 90 players, with a waiting list. It is unusual in that it has no support from government or educational sources, relying on contributions from parents, friends and other sympathetic parties, and answerable to no-one but itself. It rehearses regularly every Sunday evening during term, and usually works for a concert at the end of each term. It has adopted a regular constitution as a charitable enterprise, on a democratic basis; programmes are recommended by playing members; parents have a say in the running of the orchestra if their child should be too young to do so, and they help with some of the business arrangements. Formal auditions are held in the autumn, and regular re-auditions for string placings. The constitution states that the orchestra will attempt some works not normally in the programme of other orchestras, and there are occasional first performances. In 1975 a 'friends' organization was set up, to give financial stability, and has proved very successful, in particular for raising special finance for tours, e.g. by sponsored play-ins and book sales, for visits to Aberdeen and Sweden. Altogether, in addition to the high musical standard which is agreed by all, the orchestra gives the impression of young enthusiasm, judiciously mixed with adult experience where needed, and with a democratic approach.

Another orchestra, less ambitious but of interest because it was formed by, and is run by, young people only, is in Edinburgh – the Caritas. An ensemble was got together in 1970 for charity. By 1971 there were 50 members, and the name 'Caritas' was adopted. There is no adult administration or outside assistance; half a dozen members form the committee, and collect a subscription (currently £2) at the start of the academic year. This money, plus the proceeds from the concerts, pays for the weekly hire of hall and music, the balance going to the charity chosen. In the past, the conductors also have been of school or college age; recently, the conductorship was accepted by a professional from the Scottish Chamber Orchestra. There are probably 50 players at a concert, and quite large works are tackled – Bliss' Suite from 'Things To Come', Goldmark's 'Rustic Wedding' and the 'New World' Symphony as examples.

Several youth orchestras of high standard are organized by the Inner London Education Authority, which collects the best players from schools in its area. There is no need to go on with a list; almost every county and considerable area has its orchestra; and the varied and flexible organizations, the keen and committed membership, and the high technical standard often reached, together make a sort of musical explosion which provides music of far higher quality and quantity than was available fifty years ago.

The high standard and popular appeal of youth orchestras have been recognized by the B.B.C. – not usually enthusiastic about amateur performers – particularly in its series 'Youth Orchestras of the World', which has featured some 200 orchestras, many of which were British, in the period 1969 to 1982.

Turning now to the vocal rather than the instrumental side of youth music, one might expect that it was easier to start a small singing group than an orchestra. Almost everyone can sing to some extent; less room is needed, there is nothing expensive to buy. On the other hand, young voices have not the power or range of the adult; probably not so many young would-be conductors are interested or competent; and the music available, at least for an unaccompanied group, is much less varied. Whatever the reasons, there has not been the same dramatic increase in young singing as in playing, in the past twenty years; though quite a lot is happening. Martin Gent (one of a family of long standing at Music Camp, himself Warden of a Community College in Cambridgeshire, and recently elected as Chairman of the British Federation of Youth Choirs) summarizes the position as follows:

'Primary Schools: Probably a general decline in singing over the whole country in the last 20 years, but there are notable exceptions where there is a keen musician on the staff. The good will be better than it used to be, and there are many excellent choirs. The repertoire is considerably broader than it used to be, and many composers are writing suitable pieces for staging, often on Biblical themes.

Secondary Schools: Compulsory hymn singing almost dead! Undoubtedly there is a swing to the instrumental side. Mixed schools have to push much harder to find tenors and basses. Many schools have no four-part choir, and many only an apology for a junior choir. But there are many exceptions where there is enthusiasm and expertise available on the staff. There is expansion in choirs going to Europe and in those able to tackle a modern repertoire.

Combined School and Community, or Combined Schools: It is quite common for combinations to be formed to tackle larger works, e.g. Verdi 'Requiem' or 'Messiah'.

County Youth Choirs: Several counties now have these, e.g. Oxford, Bedford, Essex. The scale varies, but they are usually competent enough to tackle virtually the entire repertoire of 'a capella' works. A few go abroad.

Miscellaneous Youth Choirs: There are several around where individuals want to fill a gap or to run a choir. The standard is very variable, but the best is excellent.

British Youth Choir: This is over ten years old, but has only recently taken off. I suspect that the standard may be compared with that of a good County Youth Orchestra, hopefully perhaps with that of the N.Y.O.

Cathedrals: Still an important source for singers, but they tend to be insular (in my experience). Trips abroad are common for some.

Parish Churches: Dreadful decline since the War, but the outstanding exceptions remain. Trips abroad and exchanges do happen. Diocesan Festivals do continue. e.g. King's College Chapel and Ely Cathedral are used for annual occasions.

British Federation of Youth Choirs: This is a new organization, launched in February 1983. The aims are similar to those of the European Federation of Youth Choirs, the impetus having come from the Director of Education of Leicestershire. It is meant to encourage choral music in different areas through days and weekends, and particularly to serve as an organization to promote singing, as instrumental teaching has been promoted in secondary schools. Time will show!'

In general the Youth Choirs summarized above have some link with the County Music Organizers; conductors may be paid on the same basis as evening class instructors, and there is assistance for rehearsal places, music supply, etc.

'Sing for Pleasure' is an interesting movement, entirely outside the official schemes for the present; it is addressed to those who have no musical training and no obvious abilities, e.g. in sight reading; all that is asked is that they are young people who want to sing together. Consequently the style of rehearsal and of conducting is very different from that of a more sophisticated group; music is simple and is learnt by heart; there is great enthusiasm, if little technique. This movement is now registered as a charitable enterprise and will be represented on the British Federation; its activities so far have included several summer residential courses, including one for conductors.

Gerald Haigh, a Warwickshire headmaster whose main interest is choral singing, has made some forceful remarks about choirs – he is chairman of the National Association of Choirs. He says (ref. 20), 'the two nodal events of youth music-making in this country are the National Festival of Music for Youth (in July) and the Schools Prom (in November). There is a frightening dearth of good choral music (to some extent to be ascribed to the generous sponsorship by instrument firms of orchestral playing). . . . Every single adult choir must – if it does not already do so – consider its policy towards young people. It might, for instance, start a youth section, or offer a youth choir prize at a local Festival, or offer a concert platform to a school choir, or run a junior vocal workshop. There are lots of possibilities; what is unforgivable is to do nothing except complain about the apathy of the young. . . . Young musicians are amazingly free from prejudice, and will take anything from Bach to Stockhausen. Some of our best amateur choirs show the same catholicity and adventurousness of taste; some, alas, do not, and their programmes demonstrate a sad and worrying lack of vision. The choir with an inbred and static repertoire policy is running with a built-in handicap.'

Certainly to a person like myself, used to the usual range of classical and romantic music much of which I learnt in my youth, the performances displayed at the Schools Prom, when the best talent from all over the country is on show, are startling and exhilarating. I cannot myself enter wholeheartedly into brass band and rhythm music; but when I see these hundreds of youngsters doing so, with such devotion and technique, I can only conclude that it is I who am limited as a musician, rather than they; and that music in the next generation must include what these young people want if it is to flourish and be alive.

I had always thought the Ravel Quartet to be a difficult piece – but when I hear a string quartet, average age about 16, I should imagine, toss off the last movement in the Albert Hall of all places, then I must adjust myself to new standards.

About 1945 a survey of musical life in England (the 'serious' part of it, not the 'popular') was made by the Trustees of Dartington Hall (ref. 3). Considering that at the turn of the century England was described abroad as the 'land without music', it is an impressive document; solid and full of data, setting out the scene under Concerts, Orchestras, Opera, Education, the Musical Profession and the like, with a considerable chapter on Amateur Music, which is an interesting framework against which to set much of what I have described in this book. There is, of course, a good deal about the B.B.C. and its effect on the ordinary person, as regards knowledge and love of music.

But there was hardly a suggestion of what was going to happen in the next 30 years, during which the tape recorder became cheap and commonplace, and the video and the computer became part of the furniture of the home. In this 30 years, big business and modern advertising have raised the money annually circulating in the music industry into the billion range; music of a kind, whether just as an accepted background or as a focus for real attention, may accompany us waking or sleeping, working or just passing the time. There must at the present moment be more consumers of musical sound, in the widest sense, than at any previous time in history.

Indiscriminate consumption may perhaps lead in time to indigestion. But most of the musical youngsters I have been describing in this chapter are by no means indiscriminate. They are familiar with much of the finest music which exists; they are active rather than passive musicians, and their critical powers are sharpened by the discipline of trying to do things for themselves. I regard the best of them as an élite, our chief asset for the progress of music in this country. What is going to happen to them in the next thirty years? Will their interest be maintained?

A few will set their sights high, on the ultimate excellencies: and even if they fail to reach the summits, they may settle to happy and useful lives on the upper slopes of music, as professional performers and teachers. For the majority, of course, we do not know the answer. I hope that many will rejuvenate the choral and orchestral societies of their neighbourhood, will set up musical groups of their own, and will continue with their ensemble and singing groups. But there are many reasons why they may stop being active musicians, the most obvious ones being the cares of family and profession as their lives open out. And there are insidious arguments against the expenditure of time and effort in practical music. 'Why go on as an amateur in music anyway? Do you really think that amateur performance is worthwhile? Are your ears not too sensitive to tolerate it? Why not listen on your hi-fi to the latest digital recording at home in comfort? Why go out to a local concert? Above all, why bore yourself with more Kreutzer or Czerny when you will never be more than an indifferent performer? What are the attractions of a weekly rehearsal, perhaps struggling to get there through the rain? Is it not better to hear a piece of music perfectly performed than to attempt to perform it, so much less well, yourself?

It will be clear to any reader of this book that I disagree strongly with this kind of attitude, and maintain that the best way (and sometimes the only way) to understand and feel the essence of something, particularly music, is to have a try at doing it oneself. This principle, of course, cannot be pushed to extremes and would encourage the pejorative sense of 'amateurishness' to which I objected at the beginning of this book. There certainly is not time to learn even a smattering of everything in which one might be interested. But the principle I am sure is sound. I have already quoted from several distinguished people who support the 'amateur' effort; here is another passage from the now-superseded Fifth edition of 'Grove', article 'Gramophone' – written about 1950: 'The popularity of "canned" music has contributed to the decline of that domestic music-making which is the surest basis of a national's musical life. Even the most attentive listening to broadcast and recorded music can never take the place of pianoforte solo and duet playing and, above all, of the amateur chamber-music ensemble, in developing musical instincts and perceptions.'

It is the business of the young to look for new ideas; and another factor which might discourage them in developing their musical interests is the present gap between 'popular' and what could be called 'serious new' music. Samuel Pepys could pick up his recorder and play a merry jig, not essentially different in texture from the music of the 'best' composers of the period. The bawdy songs of the public house, or even the Salvation Army hymns, had much in common in their melodic and harmonic content with some of the respectable pieces published by Messrs Novello for choral societies at the end of the last century. But the majority of 'popular' music of today is noisy, monotonous, sometimes even repulsive, to him who finds his pleasure in Beethoven or Puccini, or to the rather different group who try to follow and appreciate some of the contemporary composers.

This book is based largely on personal opinions; if I may therefore put myself forward as a typical amateur of the more serious sort, I have to confess that I do not get real pleasure from contemporary music; I listen to it sometimes, or perhaps try to play it, partly from a sense of duty or exploration. Bartók is about my limit: I feel that he is a really great man, and that I can enter into much of him if I work hard enough – 'Duke Bluebeard's Castle' moves me deeply, and I can get excited by playing his first or second quartet, even with my limited amateur technique. But I have made no real attempt at anything more recent than this, and just to form a fair opinion of today's music would require more time and effort than is left to me. (I am glad to say that a number of young conductors have introduced newer works at Music Camp with success; perhaps not of the ultimate 'avant-garde', but Lutoslawski, Takemitsu and the like).

The contemporary composer will no doubt comment, 'If you and your like are not going to listen seriously to my music, then how am I to get a hearing? I write for the best technical and musical ability I can conceive: that is to say, not for the amateur. You must learn my music from professional performances and recordings.' True enough; but for most of musical history, the cleavage has not been as big as it is now, and quite a lot of the audience has been able to listen to its contemporary composers with some pleasure, and educate itself in the process. Some 20th-century composers (Britten, for example) have been able to write some of their music to include or be within the reach of, the best amateurs. Yet I have heard piano pieces which it seemed to me I could imitate well enough with a stopwatch, a hammer and a clenched fist (just as I have seen works of art on exhibition which I could have copied in my workshop very quickly with some nails, pieces of plywood, and pots of paint). I will not be so foolish as to pronounce on the artistic merits of such works (remembering the egregious mistakes of many critics in the past); but perhaps I may be forgiven for saying that I have not got time for them.

These irreverent thoughts are not to be taken too seriously; on the other side of the picture I do know of two or three small groups of excellent chamber music players (of what I would call semi-professional standard) who meet regularly to rehearse and to enjoy fully contemporary works, some in fact written for them on commission. The fact remains that most 'serious' amateurs go to their orchestra, chorus or chamber ensemble to get their pleasure from music written before, say, 1920. This cannot in the long run be very healthy for music as a whole. Can it be that the composer is not forced to think enough of his listener?

I will close this chapter with quotations from two writers of wider experience than my own:

First, Bernard Keefe. At the 36th annual conference of the S.C.A.M., he spoke about the future of music. He repeated something of what he had said in a letter to me, which I quote with his permission: 'It is clear that the cost of professional music-making is likely to increase in real terms, and at present there is little encouragement to the view that audiences will increase or be prepared to pay more for their tickets. This is partly because of ancillary costs such as transport, meals and so on, and a growing dislike of going out at night. Amateur performances encounter the same problem, though they can count on personal support. It is certainly true that the quality of such performances is often very high, and may, in my view, offer more satisfaction than the bored playthrough of a few standard classics which we often get from the professional orchestras. In the present political climate I think it unlikely that there will be any increase in public subsidy, and if the metropolitan councils are abolished there is a real threat to many musical activities.

'What then are the amateurs to do? I think they should aim at participation in community affairs, rather than imitate the pattern of professional concerts. This may mean playing often a different repertoire – fewer Mahler symphonies and more light popular music perhaps. But it would mean relating to the audience, and making a positive contribution to communal life. By this I mean playing for the disabled and handicapped; providing entertainment at the Mayor's installation; playing on remembrance days and other national occasions; playing in venues not normally associated with music, such as big supermarkets or shopping centres.'

Then in an article in 'The Times', Roger Scruton suggested that what he called 'bourgeois man' should hold the ultimate responsibility in musical criticism and culture. 'It is partly because he has been so conscious of this [i.e. Bourgeois man's] support that the modern English composer [Scruton has just mentioned Elgar, Tippett and

Britten] has written intelligible music. His work is the result of an unspoken bargain with the private man. The very same individual who sings in the village choir or plays tuba in the colliery band ... has been the spiritual guide of the modern English composer. For it is from such exemplary material that music festivals are made.' Scruton continues: 'True musical culture is an amateur activity. It is made, sustained, and criticized by amateurs, all of whom have their private tastes and accomplishments, which they willingly pool in a common pursuit of excellence.'

Scruton, subsequently attacked by correspondents for his 'complacent philistinism', 'cheerful, bustling barbarism', etc., etc., replied in a further article:

'Culture is a system of communication. There is no private culture, any more than there is a private language. Every work of Art, however personal its inspiration and however novel its form, is an act of communication, which deserves its status only to the extent that it finds or creates an audience. ... What then must the modern artist do? Surely he cannot compromise on the one major demand of his existence – the demand for authenticity, for the new bottles in which the old wine of human experience is to be served? And if bourgeois man has lost his tolerance toward innovations, is it not time to join with the minor modernists in repudiating him?

But there is a crucial distinction to be made between innovation and originality. The second, unlike the first, can never break with what preceded it ... to be original, an artist must also belong to the tradition from which he departs. To put it another way; he must violate the expectations of his audience, but he must also, in countless ways, uphold and endorse them.'

Scruton then goes on to refer to the 'Mastersingers', with its conflict between the academicism of Beckmesser and the originality of Walther. At the end, they harmonize gloriously together. The point was reinforced by another correspondent, who said, 'in the end it is not only the professional guild of the Meistersingers but also the amateur citizens of Nuremberg who decide jointly to reject Beckmesser's dead rules in favour of Stolzing's new inspiration. This is the sense in which amateurs make a musical culture.'

7
Music on Holiday

The keen musician is apt to regard his holiday as an occasion for more, rather than less, music. Perhaps with a few friends for chamber music in some peaceful spot; perhaps a family holiday where there is someone to look after the children and scope for a rather larger ensemble than he usually has; perhaps a summer school where he can get organized practice, meet new people, and have professional coaching; perhaps historic buildings and civic traditions as the focus for a Festival with good music and other things, both to take part in and to listen to – the possible variations have no limits.

I still remember with pleasure my first music holiday, with Alan Richards and his 'cellist sister Olive, in a Derbyshire cottage in 1925; good food and good quartets. And the following year, a party of a vocal quintet plus a string quartet, camping in Warbarrow Bay by the edge of the sea (before it was taken over by the Army for tank exercises), a memorable holiday when we played in the lifeboat building, and had moonlight bathing when the sea was phosphorescent as you swam – the only time I have seen this in England. The larger parties of 1927 turned themselves into Music Camp, and thereafter my holiday time was largely bespoke.

The procession of holiday makers in this Chapter is even more arbitrary in choice than my earlier selection of choral and orchestral societies, though having still the same common ground of friendship. It would seem that it needs only a strong personality or two, with access to a beautiful holiday spot, and the strong binding interest of Music, to bring together an enthusiastic group, which may well persist for many years. For example, 'Musical Adventures in Cornwall' (ref. 36) describes in a fascinating way how Maisie and Evelyn Radford built up ensemble music and amateur opera round their home at *St Anthony-in-Roseland* – could there be a more enticing name? – with few resources but their own charm and enthusiasm. This was roughly from 1930 to 1960; many of my friends used to go down regularly to Cornwall to join in their music. From about 1970, Jennet Campbell, niece to the sisters Radford, with her husband and three musical children, has lived at St Anthony and maintained similar enterprises. She says, 'We have two house parties each year – a long weekend at Easter and a week in the summer, rehearsing and playing small chamber works, culminating in a concert in the church at St Gerrans for a local charity. The numbers are usually about 12 in the Spring and up to 20 in the Summer. Accommodation is in the two cottages and a hut, rehearsals in a studio at the rear. Basically we are a strings and continuo group, ages from 14 to the late 20s, invitations go to friends of the family. We play mainly the 18th-century string repertoire, with occasional wind, but space prevents us from having a full classical wind section. For concerts we call ourselves the St Anthony Players; we try to keep the programmes attractive to all comers, and usually have a good attendance. Our main purpose is not the giving of a concert, but the opportunity to play music together in very lovely surroundings. We rehearse 5 or 6 hours a day, the rest of the time being free for other chamber music, the beach and the sea, depending on the weather. I do all the cooking and catering, and the players do the washing up. We collect a small subscription which about half covers the cost of food, etc. The fact that every year I despair of finding enough players and every year we end up with an enthusiastic team, probably has something to do with the cooking and St Anthony!'

A holiday group on a slightly larger scale is at Broneiron, in Wales, near Newtown. In 1971 John Humphries had been running 'outward bound' type courses at Brantwood, Ruskin's house on Coniston Water, and several musical friends suggested that a week should be organized to include music with the other attractions of mountain walking, canoeing, swimming, etc. This was done, and was very successful, being repeated for the next two years. It then however proved impossible to use Brantwood again, and in 1976 another suitable place was found at Broneiron; this is a Guide Conference mansion, and has housed the music party since then.

It is very much a party of families, by invitation only, covering all ages, many of whom have been regular members year by year; including many versatile musicians playing various instruments, and singing also. There is a variety of rooms suitable for ensemble playing, and the Guides help the local staff in catering. The mornings are usually for chamber music, and in the evenings there may be larger works, up to the size of an early Beethoven symphony for example, perhaps followed by more chamber music.

A large library of music for many combinations is available, and a specific programme is drawn up for each day, saying who plays what, under the guidance of a benevolent dictator – which saves a lot of time! In general there is little rehearsal, the aim being to play a lot of music through pleasantly. In the middle of this strenuous week, a day is usually devoted to climbing a neighbouring mountain, swimming, tennis and the like.

Quite a number of the 'regulars' date back to the original 1971 party; and the group now includes elements from many of the musical institutions of Ealing in London, with one or two students and some children from Chetham's or the Purcell School. The Rushton family, well known at Music Camp since its beginning, have always been prominent at Broneiron.

'Skiing with music' was for many years an unusual and successful musical holiday at an hotel in Yugoslavia, inspired and organized by Frank Hawkins; he says something about it later in this book. The day was spent in skiing (with a DIY enthusiasm extending even to the importation of a home-made ski-lift) and in the evenings the hotel, taken over for the purpose, was full of a more or less complete symphony orchestra, to the pleasure and interest of the locals!

A different sort of holiday is organized by a group having connections with the Kingston Music Club, referred to earlier. When I first knew of this holiday, it was held in the West of England, taking a hotel or boarding-house for the purpose; those who came arranged for their own catering, in the many small rooms available; it was a pleasant company, where one could walk along a corridor, knock on a door, and enquire whether there was a 'cellist within who would like to make up a quartet. In this way I first met Pru Ashbee, then hardly more than a shy schoolgirl, now one of the best 'cellists with whom I am sometimes privileged to play. In recent years this party has chosen East Anglia for its location; there will be perhaps six quartet teams, already organized; Maurice Hancock is a long-standing member of this group.

Of what are normally called 'Summer Schools' I have little experience, though to several of my friends they are a most satisfactory part of their summer music. In the early days of Music Camp, the Downe House Summer School, with some three weeks of chamber music, chorus, and orchestra, took place quite close to us at Bothampstead, and for a few years an informal cricket-match, of the soft-ball type, was a regular feature between us. Highnam Court is not strictly a 'summer school', as it offers musical and other activities all the year round. It was originally the joint effort of April Cantelo, an old Music Camp friend, and the enthusiastic amateur conductor Roger Smith. There is something of the 'stately home' in the lovely site, near Gloucester and in the opportunities it offers. At the beginning, it was very much in disrepair, and restoration has been undertaken using much voluntary labour, somewhat on Music Camp lines, but much more expensively and thoroughly, bringing the old mansion up to something like its original state. Several years ago I went down to play in the orchestra for a concert performance of Bizet's 'The Pearl Fishers', at a stage when parts of the building were still unsafe for access, electric lights were strung across on strings, and in the kitchen were to be found Music Camp cooking gear and even a chief Music Camp cook, Harlan Walker, well known at Pigotts for his splendid curries and other dishes. Things are much tidier and more sophisticated nowadays, I believe. The current 1984 brochure describes all sorts of activity, musical and otherwise, for parties up to 100 and a whole series of courses available through the year.

I have just received from old friends, Alan and Caroline Lumsden, descriptions of their week-end and holiday courses at their house, Beauchamp House, also near Gloucester; I suspect that this is a fairly recent venture, and that it is meant for young people and a more simple way of living, partly in tents and doing one's own washing up, rather in Pigotts style. Both Alan and Caroline are excellent musicians and I would think splendid with young people; for several years Alan brought his school brass band from London to Pigotts for a few days of concentrated rehearsal. I have never been to Beauchamp, but must contrive a visit there to see what is happening!

There is a bewildering variety of musical gatherings in the holidays, especially now that every flourishing youth choir or orchestra seems to have its weekend or week of rehearsal, sometimes several a year, and often residential. Also the less youthful musician is freely catered for – the British Music Yearbook for 1985 for example shows over 120 'Part-Time Training and Educational Courses', from 'Butlin's School Venture Weeks' to the 'Monastic Music Panel' or the 'Spectro-Arts Workshop', names which arouse interesting speculation. Holiday music is in fact big business nowadays.

When does a holiday group become a Festival? I suppose when it attracts outsiders as competitors or as paying audiences, perhaps adds to itself interest in other arts beside music, identifies itself with the town or region where it flourishes, and can maintain interest in a series of events rather than in just one concert. Even the Festivals of national importance must have had modest beginnings – from the charitable impulse of Dr Thomas Bisse at Hereford in 1724, or the accident of residence of a musical genius at Aldeburgh in 1948. Leaving aside these big Festivals, the number of smaller ones today is as impressive as the number of Summer Schools – again turning to that intriguing volume the B.M.Y., there are listed 240 'competitive' Festivals and about the same number of 'non-competitive' ones, implying an extraordinary total of music practised and performed, and of artists, adjudicators, and administrators engaged and paid.

Most of these will be members of the British Federation of Music Festivals, and they will often culminate in the performance of a big work by all the participants under some distinguished conductor: a pattern set originally by Mary Wakefield in the 1880s, used by Vaughan Williams at the Leith Hill Festivals which he inspired for so many years; and adopted also at the Stinchcombe Hill Music Festival which flourished in Gloucestershire between the wars.

There have been estimates that a million amateurs take part in these festivals each year, and the total effect on general musical knowledge and enthusiasm must be immense.

I have had little share in Festivals myself, though I used to play on the double-bass sometimes for Vaughan Williams at Leith Hill; and I remember taking a small and very scratch choir to compete in a Festival at Hampstead (we came top in our madrigal class, I think owing to good diction in the rapid syllables of 'Thule, the period of Cosmography'). I was impressed on that occasion by the powers of concentration of one of our basses; through the long intervals when we were waiting for our turn to perform, his head was buried in a massive book, whose title I observed to be 'Gelatine and Glue' (he was a manufacturer of confectionery when not a musician).

But there are three Festivals about which I will say something, in each case through intimate knowledge from a friend, and very different ones; St Endellion could perhaps be a much-magnified version of St Anthony, some strong personalities in a lovely place: Ashburton is a tiny singing group just bravely expanding into a small Festival; and Kendal is the legacy of Mary Wakefield and the prototype of all Music Festivals.

St Endellion Festival

I quote from a description by Rachel Evans, who has been in touch with this Festival for many years:

'There is actually a published pamphlet about its history, from the time when Roger Gaunt and Roger Waterfield took boys and girls from the East End on a social work exercise, and how it developed from there. As I remember it, the music originally grew out of this summer camp organization and took place in what is now the Rectory. When Canon Prest arrived as the incumbent some ten years later, any summer school or organization had to move out of the Rectory as Canon Prest wanted to use it for himself, and Roger Gaunt and the Committee cast round for something. They lighted on a derelict farmhouse at Trelights, formed an Arts Trust, and started the Summer Festival in a small way some time in the early seventies. The organization then grew, and Richard Hickox was asked if he would be the musical director for the Summer Festival. That then grew in about 1976, so that Fran Hickox (then Sheldon-Williams) wanted to start a Festival on her own, and the Easter Festival was born – that's the one I know most about! At the end of the pamphlet there are two impassioned pleas; one is to keep the amateur status of the Festival, and the other is that the Church should not be used for grand concerts, be they amateur or professional. At the Summer Festival, where the organization is divided, with Hickox in charge of the music, but Roger Waterfield (one of the originals) in charge of the domestic concerns, these problems show up quite considerably. At the Easter Festival, Fran and Richard run the entire thing and the difference shows in many ways.

'As to financial arrangements, the Easter Festival is entirely self-supporting, partly from the fees which participants pay, and partly from the sale of tickets at the Church, I have often wondered how the books are balanced, because a great deal is spent on publicity, and the food budget seems to be without bounds. In the summer I believe quite a few people come, paying very little, as it is Roger Waterfield's idea to give people a cheap holiday if they need it. Both at Easter and in the summer, at least a hundred and fifty people take part, some living locally, most living in lodgings arranged either by Fran or Roger, or the local St Endellion Committee. The farmhouse itself will only sleep about thirty, so the arrangement is that breakfast is provided for those living in the house. Staple foods, milk etc. are provided within the budget for those living in lodgings where they are doing self-catering, and in the house itself the cooks provide one large meal in the evening. That evening meal is the only time when everybody meets, except for the regular pub outing after the evening rehearsal, and then those who wish come back to the house for the left-overs of the day for what is known as 'carousing'.

As for the music, the rehearsals are long and tight. There isn't any real sense of personal music-making; the rehearsals are always for a public concert at the end. This is varied and exciting for the orchestral players but can be very monotonous for the singers. However, there is a magic about the place which is very difficult to define. It's partly caused by the Church being a first-class concert hall, by the eccentric personality of Canon Trent who is a good musician and obviously lives for the Festivals; there is also the feeling of isolation, that bringing music into this area particularly at Easter is an exciting adventure for everyone around. There is also the friendliness of the farmhouse. The years I have been there I have seen lonely young men and women not only get together but also thrive as personalities in a very unstructured atmosphere.'

Ashburton

In 1975 a small group began to meet privately at Ashburton in Devon, because they enjoyed singing in each other's company. A music student from Dartington wanted to try his hand at conducting; the group persisted, from friendliness as much as music; there was hardly any organization, no fees, and few expenses, a small levy providing coffee, etc. in the evenings.

Gradually standards and ambitions developed; numbers increased slightly; there were a few informal performances. Then the original conductor got married and left Devon – the group sang the Vivaldi 'Credo' at his wedding. There followed a period of uncertainty, and the group might well have collapsed at this point.

The big step was however taken of bringing in a professional, Nicholas Marshall, a teacher, horn-player (at Music Camp) and composer, who had ambitions in the development of such a group. The decision to hold rehearsals in a small hall instead of in a private house also had a big effect. Some sort of constitution was adopted, and a committee elected. The name 'Ashburton Singers' was adopted. There was some attempt at the audition of newcomers, and the restraint of one or two non-blending voices.

By 1980 the Singers had developed some local reputation, and had given a few performances. A fairly large-scale 'Messiah' was put on in 1982, with soloists and orchestra from outside. The Singers now numbered about 45, a number which it is hoped to maintain.

Meanwhile the energy of the conductor and of one or two key

personalities in the Singers was such as to promote a 3-day Festival in June 1980. This included Britten's 'Rejoice in the Lamb', and a commissioned work by Nicholas Marshall, 'Even Such Is Time', based on the life of Sir Walter Raleigh. This was a financial and artistic success, and a rather longer Festival took place the next year, with a programme of wider scope (a children's opera by Nicholas Marshall, young people's jazz group, 'Dido & Aeneas', a song recital, craft exhibitions, etc.). There was considerable local support and sponsorship, and for 1982 a regular Ashburton Festival Association was constituted as a permanent body. The 1982 plans budgeted for a turnover of around £3,000.

Altogether the Festival and its parent Singers have made a vigorous start, and might well become a permanent feature of the music of this part of Devon. There are obvious difficulties ahead, such as the small population near at hand on which to rest such an enterprise, and the present dependence on the personal energy and abilities of one or two people (one of them is Peter Beavan, who exercises his great skill as a printer most attractively in the Festival literature).

The Mary Wakefield Festival

Born in Kendal in 1853, Mary Wakefield turned from finishing school to a singing career; she had a fine voice, but the tragic death of her father determined her to return to her family base. In her late thirties she developed talents as a lecturer, feeling strongly about music as an integral part of social life and wishing to spread as far as possible the knowledge and enjoyment of music. In the summer of 1885 an embryonic competition between three vocal quartets, on the tennis lawn of her house at Sedgwick, rapidly expanded to the involvement of 140 people two years later, and over 600 in six years time. Mary Wakefield travelled widely among the village choirs, making it her aim 'to bring the greatest music within the reach of the greatest number. Musical enthusiasm is largely a gift, but it can also be cultivated, for it is very *infectious*.'

She put forward three principles which she thought important, and which remain as an essential part of many festivals today; first, that competition is an inducement to the study and practice of music; second, that prizes, as in ancient Greece, should be of symbolic, not financial, value; and third (the most original) that the contesting choirs should unite in the performance of works not included in the scheme of competitions. She felt that the combined singing of such works counteracted the narrowing tendencies of competition; and in fact this idea has become the greatest element of solidarity in the Festival movement.

By 1906 the Festival has grown into a three-day event, and was so large and expensive that it was decided to make it a biennial Festival; and so it has remained. From the time of the first visit of the Queen's Hall Orchestra under Mr Henry Wood, in 1904, orchestral playing became a regular feature in the programmes.

Mary Wakefield died in 1910, but the Festival which she inaugurated has had a vigorous life until this day, and has had a great effect on the music of Westmoreland and also of the country at large. There is a distinguished record of works performed, and of conductors and soloists engaged, and the effects of two wars, and the changes in musical climate brought about by broadcasting and the gramophone, have been survived without disaster. In the 50s and 60s the B.B.C. Northern Symphony Orchestra played regularly for the Festival, and the choral concerts were included in national radio programmes.

For many of the facts and phrases above I am indebted to John and Hazel Sumsion, old friends at Music Camp, who are closely involved in the Festival as it operates today. An important new factor has been the availability of a better hall for combined music, housing 700, plus 250 choir and orchestra.

'Previously, the combined efforts of Bingo and the Fire Officer had been a real problem over the years,' says John. In the 1983 season there was a varied programme of some 50 classes of competitors, with strong emphasis on children and schools entrants – always, in Mary Wakefield's view, an essential provision for the future development of music. Main works were 'A Child of Our Time' with the R.L.P.O. under Sir Charles Groves, and Beethoven's Mass in C with the Northern Sinfonia under Donald Hunt. In recent years, choirs have been getting larger than before, but also rather fewer in number – several in the neighbourhood have grown large enough to put on their own concerts with orchestra on separate occasions. There are also some musical leaders and teachers who believe that competition in music should be avoided; this has weakened local participation, as the Festival rules insist that all choirs participating in the concert music must also enter in at least two competition classes.

8
Financing Amateur Music

Thinking of my past experiences in music, and looking over the descriptions of amateur enterprises in this book, I realize that I have been highly privileged. I have conducted many of the greatest works of music, with good teams and in ideal conditions, without the worry of finding audiences and finding money to pay professionals. That long and distinguished line of professional singers and players who have been involved in Music Camp and its relations have given their help for the love of music alone, usually even without a small sum to cover their out-of-pocket expenses; indeed, often contributing their share like everyone else towards the inevitable expenses of the party. I do not know anyone else who has been so well treated by so many professional friends, who by their generosity have not only made higher musical standards possible, but also have contributed friendship and enjoyment to everyone.

I do trust therefore that these friends will not think me ungrateful or unappreciative if parts of this chapter criticise the financial realities in some areas of amateur music.

For the organization of amateur music, the pattern is undoubtedly changing. There is a lot more money around for leisure pursuits. The standard of the best amateurs in music is higher than it used to be, and some may reasonably enough feel resentment at the payment of fees to some 'student' professional who is obviously less experienced, and sometimes even less skilled, than themselves. (On the other hand, I know many keen amateur players, usually among those of moderate ability, who say how much they enjoy sitting next to a really good professional, brought in for the final rehearsal and concert.)

And so there grows up a class of 'semi-pros' who habitually expect quite a considerable 'expense fee'. Amateur programmes are nowadays much more adventurous, and big works are undertaken requiring full wind and expensive percussion – there is no comparison between the pair of drums (originally costing me £13) which I used to play in the old Westminster Orchestra concerts, and the many thousands of pound's worth of gleaming equipment which the best amateur percussionists of today (quite rightly) expect to have available for a concert.

Fifty years ago I tended to think that, at an amateur concert, expenses should be kept to a barest minimum, and that the total expenditure should be divided among the performers, rather than the audience (if any). This idea is perhaps no longer a practical one, except at Music Camp, where I am glad to say it is still maintained; but then Music Camp is the only fairly large-scale organization I know which is completely amateur, and it offers much more than just music to its members.

Today's organizer of an amateur group, if he is giving public concerts, must think of budgets of the order of hundreds or even thousands of pounds; and he cannot therefore disregard the channels for supplying and spending money which exist, nominally for his benefit. Vaughan Williams has said, 'Organization is not Art, but Art cannot flourish without it'. The 'official' approach is however not what most amateurs would first think of for their music, and I am sure that it needs knowledge and experience of the set-up before the best advantage can be gained from it. I always remember a remark of Sir Lawrence Bragg, about the Cavendish Laboratory, which caused delight to us senior members of the National Physical Laboratory who were listening to him – 'I always find that a big laboratory runs best on a well-rotted mulch of Administration.' Not many amateurs however have a chance of controlling the rotting of the musical mulch; they have to take what is before them, and do the best they can; for the purely amateur voice in the highest councils is, I imagine, inaudible amidst the strident orchestration of the music industry.

Sources of Funds

To start at the top, the amateur is represented at U.N.E.S.C.O., however faintly, by the National Music Council of Great Britain, whose purpose is 'to encourage and co-ordinate music in the U.K.' It is composed (1984) of 46 member-organizations, of which (roughly judged by their titles) 11 are administrative (Arts Council, county and district councils) 14 are from professional and performing interests, 10 are educational (mainly Colleges of Music), 7 represent industry and only four are likely to be concerned primarily with the amateur. It may be assumed that to this Council, 'music' means salaries, contracts, funds, copyrights, etc., rather than anything to be enjoyed.

The Arts Council is known to us all, dispensing annually some £20 million of taxpayers' money to finance opera, dance and orchestras in England, Scotland and Wales. A small fraction (some half-million pounds) is allocated to amateur societies and music clubs, hitherto mainly to help in the payment of professional fees incurred at their concerts. Until now, this assistance has been channelled through the National Federation of Music Societies (N.F.M.S.), though in 1984 the Council decided that from 1985 to 1986 onwards the disbursement of these funds should be handled by the Regional Arts Associations.

Few would question that the highest quality of opera, dance and orchestral playing should be maintained in our country, and that to do this requires public subsidy on a large scale. There could however be argument as to what proportion of funds should go directly to support amateur music; and also about the exact way in which this proportion could most usefully be spent. The charter of the Arts Council is quoted as 'to develop knowledge, understanding and practice of the Arts.' I do not know at what stage in the development of the Council's policy it was decided that this proportion, as regards music, should be spent mainly on professional fees; but it could be considered that major help in providing rehearsal and concerts rooms, in the easy provision of music, and perhaps also in the training of amateur conductors, was at least as important.

Be that as it may, in recent years very many amateur societies have relied on the N.F.M.S. to guarantee some portion of the annual losses to be expected in their budget. This aid in general has been available only to societies using professional help (as soloists, and as 'stiffening' in orchestras); if the Federation approved of the programme and the artists, it might cover 15%, perhaps 20%, of an expected deficit, depending on the past performance of the Society, and the standard likely to be reached. The society seeking aid had to be above a certain minimum size, it had to be affiliated to the Federation, it had to show that it had explored other sources of financial aid, it had to have shown a willingness toward 'self-help', which in practice meant members' subscriptions, gifts, and such money-making devices as jumble sales and benefit concerts.

These provisions seem all very reasonable ones for a body spending public money, once granted the assumption that the best way to spend it is in the provision of professional help, involving the further assumptions that this will improve the musical standard attained, and that a higher standard is the best way to increase the amateur's pleasure.

An important feature in the help given by the N.F.M.S. has been that such things as insurance and performing rights are covered at a reasonable charge, and that there are schemes for access to libraries owned by other societies. The N.F.M.S. grant has also been used to encourage the occasional performance of novel or difficult works, for which a special case can be made; sometimes grants in the £1,000s rather than the usual £100s have been made this way. It is difficult to see how the N.F.M.S., with the best of intentions to use its grants to maintain and improve standards, can form reliable views of the 'merit' of a Society. It sends some of its regional representatives to concerts to listen to them and to report; but when there are a thousand or so societies giving concerts, often more than once a year, a whole army of inspectors would be needed for a fair survey; and anyway, in my view and that of others, the average rehearsal, rather than the average concert, is what should be judged if the contribution which the society makes to music as a whole is to be assessed.

I have had no personal experience of the N.F.M.S., though I have heard criticisms on one or two other points, e.g. that too much of its money goes in the London area rather than the provinces, and also that the grant system in effect subsidises the society which buys in a good deal of professional help, at the expense of the society which struggles to bring in as many genuine and regular amateurs as possible for its concerts. I have been told that the N.F.M.S. is conscious of these and other criticisms; that it has proposed various internal changes and has been trying for a more effective approach to the introduction of new ideas, and to its potential for giving advice and support to amateur effort, as well as just financial aid.

The recent Arts Council's decision to devolve to the Regional Arts Associations the funds spent up to now through the N.F.M.S. removes from the latter its function of grant-aiding the programmes of its member societies. It seems that the R.A.A.s will in the long run have more flexibility in deciding the purposes for which grants may be used, though for the first three years the devolved funds are to be restricted to the former range of 'clients'. The other facilities the N.F.M.S. provides for its member societies (such as music exchange, performing rights cover, and insurance) will continue unaffected.

Apart from the N.F.M.S., of course, there is a complicated network of bodies and interests which can affect the amateur organizer, seeking for funds, or for advice and assistance. Some of these were well set out in the booklet 'Music and the Amateur' (ref. 4) which has interesting sections on choruses, orchestras, etc., quite apart from the question of funds. This was published in 1951, and so unfortunately is a generation out of date. I have not been able to find any current equivalent. But it seems to me that there is something which needs writing here – a report called 'Public Money for Amateur Music: where does it come from? Where does it go now? Where should it go, for the maximum benefit to music in general?'

The author of such a Report would presumably survey the Regional Arts Associations (who receive bulk grants, as we have seen, from the Arts Council, and other funds from the Education Authorities); the Local Education Authorities, particularly in the subsidies they in effect give to evening classes in music, now somewhat diminished by higher fees and greater insistence on 'residential' qualifications; and the County Music Committees with their organizers and Music Advisers.

I have no doubt that some of the efflorescence of amateur music today is due to the amount of money and help there has been around since the War. But one paragraph in the booklet mentioned above may still be apposite today, in a time of approaching financial stringency, 'there is a growing temptation [for the amateur] to sit back and rely on the Local Education Authority to provide, under the 1944 Education Act, everything that was formerly carried out by voluntary workers. If the only music groups to survive were to be those which the education authorities could and would afford to finance within their powers for further education, amateur music would be immensely impoverished.'

Historically separate from the local education network, but in fact working closely with it, are the many Rural Music Associations, which have grown largely from the pioneer work of Mary Ibberson in the 30s and 40s in Hertfordshire (ref. 26). Their original purpose was to provide music and teaching for small groups, e.g. in villages, outside the existing range of teaching in cities. There are also the Music Centres, now growing up all over Great Britain, which have a much great variety of purpose and of organization than the ordinary rehearsal-concert routine of an amateur orchestra or chorus; they are sometimes largely self-financing, are slanted towards youth and innovation, and try to link together artistic enterprise in a community, wherever found.

Support to the Music Centres has been given by the Standing Committee for Amateur Music (S.C.A.M.) which was a voluntary association of local authorities and their music committees with various amateur organizations; it grew from a joint committee for music and drama set up in 1927, with backing from the Carnegie Trust. It was not a fund-issuing body; its functions were to give advice and stimulus, organizing conferences and publications on matters of interest to the amateur – for example, the choral movement for young people, 'Sing for Pleasure', difficulties with piano tuning, purchase and hire of music, summer schools for young conductors and choir leaders, advice for fund-raising, etc. An amateur organizer will probably find stimulus in their pamphlet 'Music Matters'. Within the last two or three years, however, S.C.A.M. has been absorbed in the Amateur Music Association (A.M.A.) which, jointly with the Rural Music Schools Association, might provide a posible nucleus of an 'Independent Sector' in the organization of amateur music. Whether it has funds and determination to make any impact on the 'establishment' remains to be seen; I hope that it will not prove to be a David, challenging Goliath without a sufficiency of flints for his sling.

Many societies nowadays (like pop groups and football clubs) look for funds in commercial sponsorship; 'grants from industry and commerce' are an accepted item in the N.F.M.S. enquiries about a Society's income. When such sponsorship represents a local interest in a musical activity – as, for example, the large support given to colliery brass bands in the past – this would seem an excellent thing; but I feel that the music should come first, rather than the money. It is perhaps ominous that there is a 'Sponsorship Consultant' listed in the B.M.A. handbook, who presumably would accept amateur societies as clients. I found it a little strange also to be asked to subscribe to the funds of an amateur Rehearsal Orchestra in a normal B.B.C. T.V. charitable appeal (7 November 1982).

The Amateur and the Professional

Much could be said about the relationship of the amateur to the professional in music, particularly in regard to the professional unions, whose purpose is likely to be the improvement of pay and conditions for their members, rather than the benefit of the amateurs whom ultimately they serve.

In any skilled (or even unskilled) profession there have been strong incentives for the 'professional' to separate from the 'amateur' and to develop a monopoly, usually protective and lucrative – a guild, trade union or 'closed shop' often backed by legislation or 'sanctions' against those who disregard its rulings or privileges. This is to be expected where the consequences of incompetence are irreversible or perhaps even fatal, as in Law and Medicine; but not so justifiable in all departments of modern life: the D.I.Y. movement may perhaps be seen as the ordinary man's protest against the incompetence of many carpenters, electricians or plumbers.

I have not heard of 'unions' to control the output of writers, painters, or composers, though the mechanism for such a control for the written word appears to exist already in the 'chapels' of Fleet Street, should printers ever concern themselves closely with the content of what they print! But the music once written, its performance, and its subsequent recording or broadcasting, is much subject to union action. As in other occupations where big money is involved, there has been a growing tendency to restrict paid musical performance to the union member, as represented by the Musician's Union and by Equity.

The amateur performer of music is in an unusual position, compared with those engaged in many other activities – first, he enjoys his occupation and needs no financial incentive to make him continue it; and second, a great part of Music as it exists at any moment depends on his activity, independent of any professional help. Without the professional, the listener would have no celebrity concerts, and might perhaps get tired of his old recordings, the typical amateur concert might become restricted in programme and lose the bloom of first-class soloists, but much could survive; very different from the likely results, were all doctors to go on strike to protest against the amateur's dosing himself with aspirin! I suspect too that brass bands, a good deal of 'pop' music, and some amateur opera would get on very well for a time without assistance.

This may read as if I was trying to depreciate the value of the professional musician. Nothing could be further from my intention. Music depends, past, present and future, on that handful of precious people who are creative composers and interpreters of the first rank. They set the standards at which we others impossibly aim; they encourage us amateurs to do, in our humbler way, as well as we possibly can; they lay a corner-stone in that lovely edifice in which we, perhaps, do a little filling-in. And round them there must be a corps of fine musicians, not perhaps in the first rank, but far more skilled than we could possibly be. But as we descend the mountain-peak of real distinction, do we perhaps find the lower slopes too densely inhabited?

Each year there is a flood of students passing through the Music Colleges, most of whom at one stage probably intend to make music their full-time occupation. Excellent: but at the full fees demanded by the Unions, is there work for them all? May it be that the Unions are cutting their own throats, at least as far as the younger and less well-established members are concerned, by their attempts at such high minimum fees?

I have already said (in Chapter 4) that the proportion of income spent by some societies on professional fees seems excessive, when we consider the purpose for which those Societies were originally formed, which was *not* the support of the musical profession! Matters would be much easier if the Unions would accept the fact, already stated in this Chapter, that a young student fresh from his Academy is often (for the purposes of an amateur concert) no better than the best amateurs, and is worth only a small fee. Is not a two-tier system a possible answer, which would distribute the money which an amateur body can afford in a more equitable and productive way? Of course, many young players do in fact make adjustments, and bend the rules on occasions, but this should not be necessary. The whispered enquiry 'are *you* being paid for this?' sometimes circulating in amateur orchestras at the final rehearsal, is very divisive, and can lead to trouble.

I have been speaking so far mainly of the orchestral player; there is no doubt that the amateur orchestra cannot in general take the place of the professional body in the performance of music, and also that often it really needs professional help in the right quarters for its own concerts. But things are not quite the same with choral music.

Generations of amateur singers have shown that, given enough rehearsal and an inspiring conductor, they can perform the larger works of music in a first-class way, as in fact their composers presumably conceived them; and even more difficult works of the unaccompanied repertoire can be given finished performances by picked teams of amateurs. As I have already said in this book, the problems are simpler and fewer; a year's training in ensemble singing will not produce a Ferrier or a Shirley-Quirk, but it can well develop, with a gifted amateur, enough technical control to meet the demands of an exacting conductor of a choral group.

This being so, it is disconcerting to find that over the past twenty years there has been strong pressure from the actor's union (Equity) to resist any collaboration by their members, i.e. young professional singers, in public performances, recording, B.B.C. activities, etc., where the main body is amateur. This is particularly unfortunate for some of the smaller choral groups which have originally been formed to give good performances of unaccompanied works, or larger works in 'chamber' conditions probably similar to those envisaged by the composer. The result has been that sometimes these groups have had to disband, or modify their structure and purpose; in either case, depriving some good amateur singers of the opportunity of singing to a high technical standard. I have been advised however that it would not be politic for me to give any details, from the many I have heard in conversation; I personally have not been concerned with any such Union action, nor has the music which I have organized suffered in any way.

And what of the B.B.C.? Here the official face is firmly set against admixture of amateur with professional, largely from the Union attitude, but also because of the justified opinion that for most music the highest possible standard demands professionals throughout (excepting of course the big choruses). If amateurs appear, it is in such excellent series as 'Youth Orchestras of the World' or 'Choir of the Year' (where fantastically good performances may be heard on occasion). It would certainly be disastrous to offer the average amateur performance to the B.B.C. listener instead of a professional one, in general. Yet in view of the enormous volume of amateur playing which exists, some of which is worth listening to purely on its own merits, it is perhaps a pity that no programme corner seems to exist for the regular display of the best amateur examples, if only 'pour encourager les autres'.

9
Thirteen Variations

One recurrent theme in this book is the question, 'Why do we do music?' I rather naïvely imagined that by putting it to a handful of my friends and asking for a reply – 'no more than 400 words, please' – I could derive an interesting chapter for this book with some unusual and thought-provoking answers. I was sadly mistaken; I assembled a bulky file of some 7000 words, with intriguing and varied accounts of musical experience, but hardly any coherent attempts at answering my question as such. Nevertheless, with drastic compression and omission (for which I hope my correspondents will forgive me) I felt that the result was worth presenting in this book. I leave it to my readers (some of whom will know many of the original writers) to fill in the gaps.

Edgar Fuchs has had a bigger share in playing and organizing chamber music than most of us. As the son of Carl Fuchs, distinguished professor of the cello and principal in the Hallé Orchestra, and of a mother who was a professional pianist, he was in a musical atmosphere from the start – 'when I was five years old, without any great enthusiasm I took for granted that one practised a bit each day, one learned about keys and played their scales, major and minor, and little pieces until one no longer needed the music.' But he found strings more attractive than the piano, and at nine started on a small violin, with excellent teaching from his aunts. His main schooling started at 13 at the Manchester Grammar School – here music was quite well encouraged, but only as a 'fringe' subject, with limited time available – much less than it would be allotted at the same school nowadays. Edgar helped to run the school Music Study Circle (including lectures and recitals from outside the school), and meanwhile had chamber music at home 'in full swing'.

Then came Cambridge (where he and I arrived at the same moment, were given the same test piece for sight reading by Dr Rootham, and met at the first rehearsal of the season of the Cambridge University Musical Society). There was lots of music, and an early introduction to Music Camp. In 1928, with Philip Lewis, he

started the 'Double-Fisters' group (cf. chapter 3); he married a
'cellist wife, and met **Philip Godlee**, an influential and energetic
amateur player, with whom he played quartets till his death ... 'a
regular quartet, led by a very French lady, Simone Wenner, one of
those perfect soloists with no idea of what chamber music is really
about, but luckily amenable to all suggestions from "below".'

The Bangor Summer School, with Keswick Hall and Dartington,
gave good playing and coaching, and acquaintance with first-class
players. Edgar in 1946 started a Music Section at Winnington Hall
Club, for monthly concerts, lectures and recitals – this is still flourishing, nearly 40 years later.

The U.S.A. also brought many chamber music contacts. One day
a sergeant appeared at Edgar's house in Knutsford, saying, 'if I
don't get some chamber music in the next 48 hours, I think I shall
die.' They managed a couple of sessions for him before he vanished
in three days' time with Patton's troops to land on D-Day on the
Normandy beaches. He turned out to be Jo Stein, later President of
the Amateur Chamber Music Players of the U.S.A. referred to
earlier in chapter 5. Twenty years later, Jo turned up for more music,
and there was a return when Edgar visited the U.S.A., cramming 58
different works (he says) in the intervals between his professional
visits to various engineering firms. On a later visit he met Helen Rice
and many other good players who have made reciprocal visits to
England in their turn.

Edgar says finally, 'Once a keen amateur, one is that for life, even
if stiff fingers and poor hearing prevent one from playing. Writing
programme notes for our chamber music series is still an interesting
and congenial occupation.'

Frank Hawkins writes: 'My father, an amateur violin and viola
player, was one of five brothers all amateur string players (two
violins, viola, and two cellos, like the Schubert string quintet). He
was for many years treasurer of the South Place Sunday Concerts,
and my mother was also on the committee, later becoming assistant
Secretary. This meant that from a very early age I was exposed to all
the best string quartets and chamber music ensembles. (The organization of the Concerts is entirely voluntary, a labour of love by
amateurs. In 1969 the 2,000th concert was reached, and I wrote an
account of them in 'The Story of 2000 Concerts'). This background
(also the availability of my father's instrument) was the inspiration
for me to study the viola, which I did at the Royal College of Music,

with horn as second subject. (Ten years earlier Livia Gollancz had studied the same instruments with the same professors at the same place; it was she who introduced me to Music Camp, for which I am eternally grateful.) If I had been a good enough viola player I should have liked to have been in a professional quartet, but I wasn't, so the horn overtook the viola and I worked as a professional horn player for over 20 years. But I continued to play the viola as an amateur. During this time I was very active in the Musician's Union and later became interested in printing (also inherited, I suppose – my father worked for Waterlow's).

'In 1959 I went skiing with Alan Pollard and we both agreed that skiing was wonderful, but we missed chamber music in the evenings. So we decided to get a quartet together and go skiing. When 24 people presented themselves – a chamber orchestra – the Skiing and Music Society was born. It made annual visits abroad, for skiing during the day and music-making in the evenings, until 1973. The fall in the pound and my own income as a horn player meant that I could not carry on organizing S.A.M.S., so in an effort to restore my ailing finances in 1976 I got a job in Austria as a viola player. I regard this period of my life as a re-training period. In 1979 I moved to the orchestra in Bad Wiessee in Germany, also as a viola player, but with a contractual obligation to play horn when required – probably a unique job for my rather unusual qualifications.

'I am not averse to taking money for playing the viola, but the sort of work we do, mostly 'good light music' in a small ensemble, is just like chamber music and I approach it in just the same way as my amateur quartet playing. I now regard myself as a horn player who loves playing string quartets.'

Rachel Bowles writes: 'I've always sung – at 5 years I had aspirations to sing "Maisie Dotes" (a seaside comedy song) on the stage at a Sunday School treat, ending in confusion as my Mama walked in at the back! A crucial point came at 12 with our new organist. The choir, a typical Yorkshire Methodist choir, needed fresh blood, and the best of the juniors were brought into choir practice, taught a little bit initially on our own to get the hang of chanting, and then expected to make our own way. The challenge of improving one's sight reading, or making sure that one was 'with' Miss Ellam, our chief soprano, and not behind, and a diet of Samuel Wesley, Stanford, Stainer, Handel and Mendelssohn sent a well-founded chorister up to University to sing with Thornton Lofthouse and the London University Music Society. A move to Hull University added some skill in madrigal singing as well as larger choral works. Back in London, this was continued at the Institute of Education and the Latymer School. Then a new opportunity – the Saltarello Choir, run as an evening class for Nicholas Braithwaite to conduct us. This was no ordinary choir – each voice was above average in ability and musicianship, and within a term it developed into a completely amateur cantata choir capable of producing a good programme with about six rehearsals.

'My job then took me north again, to south-west Lancashire, where there was little difficulty in joining a madrigal group and then the Liverpool Cathedral Singers and the Philharmonic Choir for the big stuff. Over the next four years I worked with other college choirs as well as my own, including some solo work, and also with a small newly-formed choir at Formby. But here troubles began to arise with the pro/amateur relationship. The conductor of this choir was enthusiastic and did his work for love, and his friends, some from the Liverpool Philharmonic, came and played and sang solos enjoyably, without fee. But then the leader asked for a fee, feelings were aroused, and it became apparent that there would soon be no professional players playing for love – their Union would see that it was not possible.

'The habit of paying fees was developing. Called in 1967 to do the contralto solos in the 'Messiah' for a college concert, I was astounded to find later a cheque in the post for my trouble, and was told that it would be impolitic to refuse it. This fee-paying habit, together with the tendency for young singers to leave home to find work, and the dwindling congregations, helped to diminish the oratorio tradition in the chapels of the Welsh Pennine valleys; funds were not sufficient to pay four soloists of quality. Yet it used to be the proud boast of all the valleys that they had amateur voices who had sung without embarrassment with Isobel Baillie and others of her stature.

'In 1968, on returning to London, I attempted to build up a musical life similar to the one I had in Lancashire. College choir, solos and scratch singing were not difficult to find. I did not join a big choral society because of shortage of time, with marriage and a new job; but there was a good cantata choir nearby, similar in purpose to what I had enjoyed in Liverpool, i.e. competent to prepare for a good concert in half-a-dozen rehearsals. But I found that its make-up was very different – its core was a group of young professionals just out of or about to leave college, who did all the small-scale singing; genuine amateurs were only needed for the big events. I have found this to be generally true – the abundance of under-employed professionals in London has pushed out the keen local amateurs who want something better than the typical evening institute choir.

'I have found only one sphere in music (outside Music Camp) where the top professional mixes with the amateur on something of an equal footing – that of the organ recital world. Perhaps here it is the nobility of the instrument, probably with an individual history, which binds together everyone with knowledge and enthusiasm, without question of fee.'

One might expect a new daughter-in-law to have a big influence in Music Camp circles; and *Rachel Wheeler Robinson* (nee Verney) comes from a numerous and distinguished family of practising musicians. It was interesting to ask her to formulate what were, to her mind, the essential differences between the amateur and the professional in music; from a point of view less obvious than that of my first chapter.

From the earliest age, she grew up with family music round her; a clan of uncles, aunts and cousins would sit round and sing madrigals, the youngsters being encouraged to listen, but to join in only when their musical technique had become adequate. A whole repertoire of rounds and canons was expected of the children; with Rachel at the piano, traditional songs and hymns were known to all, and there was the church choir, with which she was an occasional deputy organist. As she grew older, there was a strong tendency towards the professional approach; an uncle and an aunt married professional musicians, one sister is now a cellist of distinction, the other a singer and accompanist with a serious approach to music; three cousins are professional players. Besides the piano, which was her chief instrument at the R.C.M., she fell in love with the violin at an early age, but this was spoilt for her by unsympathetic teaching. After the R.C.M. she was considering a career as an accompanist, but she formed a strong interest in music therapy, particularly for the handicapped, and for the past ten years this has been her chief occupation. The first distinction she would make between the professional and the amateur would be the obvious one of technique. Most amateurs cannot develop their full potential as musicians through lack of technical skill. But beyond this, and accepting that some amateurs today are remarkably proficient in technique, a more profound difference lies in their attitude of mind. Is the purpose of music to give a maximum of enjoyment, accepting the limitations of occasion, available time, and technique? Or is compromise to be rejected in search of a higher perfection?

Much of the music in Rachel's life has been in the first category – though often of high quality, it was for fun, for immediate enjoyment. But there exists for her a higher plane of musical experience which is more precious, where no allowances are made, where every detail is examined, discussed and rehearsed, where the aim is the best that can be conceived. She can enjoy the happy dashing-through of some great work, as one kind of pleasure; but it is in the long run more satisfying to her to work with this higher aim in mind, demanding reserves of technique, and great patience and devotion. This is to her the ultimate difference between amateur and professional, an attitude of mind occasionally displayed by exceptional amateurs; she instanced a particular performance of the César Franck Violin Sonata at Music Camp, by two gifted 'amateurs' who had this attitude, both at rehearsal and at performance.

Memorable moments in music of course come sometimes under either category. She described a performance of a Bach Flute Sonata which she would always remember as having something of perfection; and on the other hand, a family group which climbed a Welsh mountain under her father's direction, in the mist; at the top they sat down and sang a Tallis 8-part canon. Out of the mist there appeared the ecstatic face of an American soldier, who said, 'When I suddenly heard that, I thought for a moment that I had died and gone to Heaven.'

For a year Rachel worked in Denmark as a music therapist. She found there no tradition of amateur music, nor for that matter was there a high standard of professional playing. She then worked for some years in Germany, starting perhaps with some prejudice against amateur music in general. But contact with one or two very good amateurs there, and the passport which her piano playing gave her into people's homes, rather modified her views. She now feels that one of the virtues of amateur music, particularly in England, is that the music itself takes the first place, and that personal jealousies and ambitions are unimportant.

Peter Dungey writes: 'I was fortunate to have parents both of whom loved music – piano and singing. When I was about eight years old my father taught me to play the E flat tenor horn. My musical horizons were quickly extended: I had lessons on euphonium and trombone from the bandmaster at Clifton College, who, with my father, was serving in the Territorial Army. So I joined the same regiment as a musician. I played with the Bristol Light Opera Company, and discovered Gilbert & Sullivan and other operettas.

'In 1939 the regimental band was disbanded; I drove a tank till I was wounded in 1942 and became a P.O.W. – with musical starvation. Home again, I bought a trombone and played in a brass band in Bristol. I have vivid memories of my first brass band contest – held in gale force wind and rain in a field in Cornwall. The test piece was an arrangement of Beethoven's Fifth Symphony; to ensure impartiality, the adjudicator was shut away in a tent. He may have kept dry, but I am sure he had difficulty in hearing the bands through the storm!

'But although I enjoyed brass banding, my main musical interest was in the orchestra, and in South Wales I played in many pit orchestras and choral and orchestral concerts. The first time I heard and played the Fauré "Requiem" in St Mary's Church, Swansea, was an unforgettable experience.

'In 1963 I was moved to Gatwick Airport and we bought a house in Crawley. I made many musical contacts, and quickly realized that my trombone, an old small-bore Courtois, was inadequate. Despite the morgage we found the money to buy the best possible replacement – a Conn 88H in B flat/F, a very fine instrument which I still play. Inevitably my musical interests broadened – listening to chamber music brought me great pleasure, but I was frustrated because I was not involved myself – there was no brass equivalent. So, inspired by the Philip Jones Brass Ensemble, three friends and I formed the Hill Brass Ensemble, a quartet of two trumpets and two trombones, and our first public appearance was at a Music Competition at Horsham – winning our section with two Gabrieli Canzonettas was a stimulus. We progressed, developing a flexible programme with various brass combinations; and we endeavoured to trace the development of brass instruments and music from the Gabrielis, Lassus, Holborne, Locke through to modern works by Arnold and Horowitz. We also provided the brass section for various 'shows', and with the money we earned we built up a reasonable library. Shortage of music for brass was still a problem (it is much improved in recent years), so an attempt at making my own arrangements seemed to be a partial solution. But keyboard knowledge was essential, so I started having piano lessons.

'Then in 1971 I was invited to Music Camp. I was rather shaken by the high standard of musicianship and instrumental technique. But it stimulated me into a long period of study, culminating in a teacher's L.R.A.M. diploma.

'In 1982 I retired from the Civil Service, increased my teaching activities, and also attended Trinity College of Music as a part-time student. From being an enjoyable hobby, music has become a rewarding and fascinating second career.'

Arthur Radley describes 'Sixty Years of Choral Singing':
'I was born into music. My father sang a neat "Down in the Forest" and led us in improvised rounds on country walks; my mother, an ex-R.C.M. pupil, taught piano and 'cello. When I was eight, I took the tram every Wednesday to Stockport for the Co-op Choir; we rehearsed literally under the arches of the great railway viaduct, and so good was my grounding in Tonic Sol-Fa that it accompanies every tune I sing in my head still. My first public performance was Elgar's "The Snow", as tear-jerking then as now. At school I got top marks for my Sterndale Bennett's "Spring"; or was it for my first public appearance in long trousers? Hymn singing periods were compulsory, even in a Quaker school – the best grounding, surely, for part-singing. The inspirational seal was set by a visit to the Music Camp in the Great Barn at Hope Farm, Audley End, in 1933, when I was 17; my next Camp was not till the 100th in 1981, but I "reunioned" in London, on and off, for some 30 years, a privilege.

'My first real regular choral singing was with the Oxford Bach Choir, 1935–1938. We rehearsed in Ruskin's Museum, and my first sight of the Heather Professor of Music, Tommy Armstrong, was from way up, whence he looked exactly like the kid in the Cow & Gate adverts – that cherubic countenance with just a wisp of blond hair sticking out. His smile in the opening bars of Haydn's "Seasons" – "Come, Gentle Spring" – was an induction into Heaven. But the times were out of joint for such a "frivolous" work in the mourning for George V, and I had to learn the Brahms "Requiem" at a week's notice: no problem for the older hands from the Town, but the best of practice for a raw student. Tommy brought in his predecessor, Sir Hugh Allen, who patted the soprano on her back after her performance, in public in the Sheldonian. At rehearsal he had turned to the lugubrious baritone from the Cathedral Choir and just said, "Sir, do you think you could possibly sing it as if all were not lost?" We got back to the "Seasons" later all right, followed by Vaughan Williams' "Sea Symphony", some Parry which moved us particularly since Tommy revealed its comfort to the Choir in the dark days of the First War, the "St Matthew Passion", and "Singet dem Herrn" in St George's Chapel, Windsor. My last with this choir was the "Missa solemnis" in 1939; with war clouds gathering again, we all asked ourselves when we would sing it next.

'I had one spell with the professionals. I was B.B.C. T.V. Music Organizer 1960–1965, the "backroom boy" fixing studios, contracts, budgeting and the like. My annual "perk" was Front of the House for the B.B.C. special relay from Glyndebourne; I had to get the invitations out, and enjoyed a remarkable burst of popularity in the run-up weeks!

'In recent years I have never been a rehearse-every-Wednesday singer, but I have sung pretty well everything I wanted to sing – and conversely (and this is the fun of being a freelance) very little that I didn't. The real joy lies in trying not to let the others down, working at one's own breathing, tone and attack, and just getting it right so that you can say to yourself "that was a real performance, and I was part of it".'

Simon Routh is a civil servant, also an excellent violinist. He writes: 'Music is almost unique in that it is a worthy profession, but can also be a totally absorbing hobby. This does depend to a large degree on location, and in this sense London is remarkable in the spectrum of amateur music that is available. I would go further and say that there is a danger in becoming a professional in doing what perhaps one enjoys most in life. By keeping music as a hobby this danger is avoided, and, depending on location, one is able to achieve enough playing (or singing) of a sufficiently high standard to satisfy one's urge for music making, whilst pursuing a career in a suitably diverse subject.

'In London, in particular, this opportunity is readily available. There are numerous orchestras, of which I play regularly in five – Chelsea Opera, Hertfordshire Chamber, Tallis Chamber, Salomon, Informal Chamber – but there are many, many more. There are also a lot of "one-off" concerts/shows, consisting either of one rehearsal and concert, or a show lasting over a week. That, very briefly, summarizes the "organized" music I am involved in in London. The particularly enjoyable aspect is that, while the name of the group may change, many of the people who play seem to remain the same. It is therefore rare if one doesn't know a majority of the players in any orchestra one plays in within this circuit.

'What about chamber music in this idyllic framework? Here I may

be pontificating to the converted; for I believe that in essence, unlike
the larger scale music making I have just described, chamber music
is for the individual(s) to arrange and organize – and others are more
able than I at that! I probably play in about one (or, if lucky, two)
quartets a week, but not usually in preparation for a concert – simply
for fun. The problem I personally find with this form of music-
making, in my present circumstances, is that it does involve more
organization and is therefore more difficult to fit in with a full-time
job – but it promises great things for the future!

'Having outlined my general experience I would emphasize my
main contention, that music can (and should) be enjoyed on an
amateur basis rather than as a professional. Those groups I enjoy
playing with most (excluding Music Camp) are the ones like the
Hertfordshire Chamber Orchestra which rehearse for one weekend
(often residential) and perform one or two concerts the following
weekend. This enables one to decide whether or not to play in a
concert without having to commit oneself to rehearsals on a weekly
basis. I would conclude by saying that, without exaggeration, there
is enough organized music in and around London at a reasonably
high standard for a good string player to have a choice of at least two
things to play in any night of the week (including Sundays) – the
problem is to limit the playing one does.'

Geoffrey Hartley grew up in a family which had much domestic
music, linked with the very cultured and artistic society of Boar's
Hill, Oxford, in the 1920s. As a boy, he learnt to play on a Savory
(French) bassoon from his father's collection of old wind instruments, and began to build up a wide orchestral experience in the
Harrow School orchestra, the Oxford Orchestral Society and the
Radley College orchestra. Eventually he changed over to the German system (Heckel) and acquired a knowledge of most wind
instruments, which he began to teach at Bryanston School. He
became an A.R.C.M. on bassoon in 1931, and made a reputation as
soloist, e.g. with the Mozart concerto, with many amateur orchestras.

He became skilled at arrangement and composition, especially of
works for special occasions and needs, some of which were published
and have received many performances; concertos for 3 bassoons, or
for 'a superfluity of flutes' for example, and what he christened
'Minicantatas' – a kind of tiny Gilbert & Sullivan operetta, usually
centred on some well-known limerick and taking only 10 minutes to

perform. In the 1939–45 War he worked at the Meteorological Office, and conducted its choir; for many years he conducted the Woking Orchestral Society, and played with the Chelsea Opera Group and the Informal Chamber Orchestra. In 1948, together with Ann Channon, he formed the Occasional Wind Players, still a flourishing body (described earlier in this book). He has much increased the number and importance of his father's collection of old wind instruments.

His first wife was a flautist, his second a violinist; his daughters and several grandchildren are excellent musicians. Altogether, throughout his life, he has been an active and distinguished centre of amateur music, particularly for those concerned with woodwind playing.

I talked with *Brian and Rosalind Richards*, son and daughter-in-law of Alan Richards, already mentioned in this book. Brian is a surgeon living near York; both are singers of ability, he a good clarinet player and she a trained teacher and performer on the violin.

First I enquired about musical family holidays. Both Brian and Rosalind were for several years members of the group at Prussia Cove in Cornwall, run by the Tunstall-Behrens family, and centred on a big house, with cottages around, and a magnificent music-room looking out over the sea. Fifteen or so families used to live in the cottages, catering for themselves; the musical standards were high, and several young conductors (Roger Norrington, Howard Williams, Robert Anderson, for example) directed the music. The beautiful site, the friendly family atmosphere, and the warmth of spring in Cornwall could sometimes produce a real ecstasy of enjoyment. On one occasion at a concert in Truro Cathedral Sándor Végh joined the party, to play the Beethoven Violin Concerto; listening to some casual wind playing he said, 'you would never get amateur playing of this quality in Germany.' But after several years the original amateur spirit was somewhat diminished; Végh and his pupils developed the master-class approach, and Prussia Cove continues today on rather different lines.

We then talked about the choruses and orchestras at present in York, and the emphasis was on the problem of the poor player, often a long-standing and most devoted member, in an orchestra which wants to raise its standard and attract better players. There seems to be no solution to this awkward problem. One York orchestra was discussed in detail; it had for years been declining in standard, but a new conductor, an excellent and hard-working man, brought in an ex-professional leader and did his best to improve things. Gradually the first violins as a body developed something of a corporate sense, came regularly to rehearsals, took lessons, and practised, with a notable improvement in the general string sound, an improvement which spread also (by imitation) among the wind players. But after a couple of years it became obvious that there were many players in the seconds and violas in particular who had no hope of significant improvement. The conductor was urged to institute auditions and be ruthless in removing players who could not improve; but he refused, his argument being that human values were more important here than purely musical ones.

There is an excellent chamber choir in York, the Chapter House Choir, of some 35–40 voices. When, a year or so ago, the founder, Andrew Carter, decided to retire, the vacant conductorship was widely advertised; some 45 applications for this unpaid job were received, in some cases stating a readiness to move house from distant parts. There are many other choral opportunities at York – at the other extreme of technique, for example, there is a male voice choir where few can read music and everything has to be learnt by heart, almost note for note; yet the results are excellent and the keenness remarkable.

Jack Waddell is a teacher, a keen and experienced oboe player, and a useful chorus member. He had musical parents – his father was a music critic and organist, his mother had a clear and accurate singing voice. He never acquired much keyboard skill, though he had lessons on the piano for most of his childhood; but he sang a lot and heard much music at school; he was not attracted by the oboe when he first heard it as a youngster. He had an active musical life at Cambridge, and started teaching in 1950; he organized at King's, Canterbury, a Madrigal Society which still flourishes. At about this time his father presented him with a rudimentary oboe with three more or less unusable reeds. 'I realized that when I played in the orchestra, the many other players who began to look round were not doing so because of the beauty of sound or the excellence of intonation.' Things got better with another instrument and contact with some first-class players; lessons from McDonagh and success as a reed-maker led to wider orchestral experience, as at summer schools (Canford, Queenswood, Downe House). Jack went to teach at Aldenham in 1954; he played in the Watford and St Albans orchestras, the old London 'Senior' under Ernest Read, and (now for many years) in the Royal Amateur Orchestral Society, meeting many young players who went on to a professional career. He was a founder member of the Edinburgh Rehearsal Orchestra under Harry Legge, and played as principal with the Polyphonia Wind Music Society under Brian Fairfax, 'who was in a sense competing with Leslie Head and the Kensington Symphony Orchestra to lay on the biggest first performances – I think we won, with the first public performances in England of Mahler's Third Symphony and Havergal Brian's "Gothic".'

Jack came first to Music Camp in 1962. 'I liked the serious attitude to music, chamber as well as orchestral, and also the involvement of every one in "chores" – I was lucky at that Camp in being an "incinerator" together with Frank Butterworth, who also instructed me in the gentle art of playing billiards. The happy result of that Camp was that I joined the "Skiing and Music" party run by Frank Hawkins at Podkoren in Yugoslavia – I was hopeless at skiing, but enjoyed the music and the company, and went on many other S.A.M.S. trips.'

Jack stresses very much the way in which the amateur wind player depends on having a good instrument and good reeds, if he is at all to approach the professional, with his constant practice and playing. Only seldom can an amateur be at his best. It sometimes requires real courage to conquer nerves. Yet to play with really good players (as once, for example, deputizing at a rehearsal of the Haydn Concertante with Amaryllis Fleming, Parikian, and Gwydion Brooke) may give an illusion of ease in dynamics and intonation not, alas, permanent.

At Aldenham School he regularly arranges midsummer Serenade Concerts, where boys can come and lie on the grass and revise for exams while listening to music. Jack also organizes late November concerts with the 'Aldenham Chamber Orchestra', a scratch group that rehearses and plays on one afternoon and evening. Finally Jack says, 'I have often wondered whether anyone has the right to be paid for playing music. Should we not simply return to the Elizabethan ideal that all gentlemen and gentlewomen should naturally be able to sing and play?'

I was fortunate in finding two old friends, both excellent professional cellists, in conversational mood after a chamber music weekend together. I got the talk going with one or two questions:

BWR: 'Why do you enjoy music, such as the Beethoven quartet we played together this morning, when you could undoubtedly collect players of a higher technical standard than myself, for instance?'

Pru Ashbee: 'Well, in some ways it is like a chance to re-read a favourite book. I love the music – I want to experience it again. Listening to a recording, technically perfect though it may be, is not at all a substitute.'

Peter Beavan: 'I, too, just like the music, and would accept the simile of reading a well-known book again. When playing, I hear the music as much in my mind as in my ear; I am thinking of it all the time; I can, if need be, switch off some kinds of critical faculty and disregard some kinds of technical weakness.'

Pru: 'I find that the main essential for my enjoyment is musical understanding, and the inter-reaction of the players; and quite often the pro group is not as good as the best amateur one in this respect.'

BWR: 'It could be argued that the high standard of finish in, say, a modern quartet playing Haydn is irrelevant and unnecessary, since the composer never heard, nor presumably imagined, it like that.'

Pru: 'The good performers in Haydn's day must have been people with the same musical potentialities as ourselves; technically things may have changed, but the overall musical effect may be very much the same.'

Peter: 'It is what you put in to it that matters, not so much what the composer had in mind or directed; and in one sense a good amateur team can put in as much as a professional one.'

Pru: 'Technically there has been a lot of progress this century. And nowadays, too, there is the interesting trend towards "authentic" performance.'

BWR: 'Have you taken part in any such?'

Pru: 'Personally, not often; but I find them interesting, e.g. in early piano trios, where the musical balance (e.g. low notes on the fortepiano against the cello) is more satisfactory.'

Peter: 'I personally find little pleasure in "authentic" performances. I think that Bach would have revelled in a modern Steinway Grand, and I prefer the D Minor Concerto, or even the Goldberg Variations (with their two-manual writing) when played on such an instrument. It seems to me that there is a new dimension of emotion and feeling thus opened up.'

Pru: 'Certainly I think that some mixtures of old and new are to be avoided – a cellist playing continuo being doubled on a modern piano for example.'

Peter: 'To return to the amateur/pro comparison, to me the purpose of a real performance is to arouse emotion in the listener; and granted a sufficiency of technique, it is musical insight which counts, and the amateur sometimes displays this better than many professionals. On the other hand, the top experiences in music, to me, have been the few occasions with conductors of the highest rank – Beecham, Giulini, Klemperer – and a fine orchestra, where all has gone well. No amateur conductor can reach these heights. The average professional small group, and its director, usually have sound competence but no particular distinction. I have in general had just as much fun from good amateur as from professional performances, with the exception of the special occasions of musical experience to which I have referred.'

BWR: 'One difficulty in amateur music-making is the bringing in of professionals as "stiffeners" and soloists. To many (such as yourselves in some stages of your careers I imagine) this is an important source of income. But do you consider that an amateur society which spends say 75% of its income on professional fees can be described as "amateur"?'

Peter: 'Usually the only way to keep an amateur orchestra together is to give it a concert as a goal to work for; and without some professional help the standard could be disastrously low. In Totnes, for example, there is a keen orchestra run by an amateur conductor who is a good musician (also a composer) and who works hard to include as many people as possible in the orchestra – even to the extent of writing special parts for some of limited technical ability. He aims at three concerts a year, each with three rehearsals. But without some help his players would not get enough musical satisfaction to stick together.'

Pru: 'At Bangor, a coherent body of players, of the standard say to be found at Music Camp, simply does not exist.'

Peter: 'Audiences for amateur concerts would of course fall off if the standard was too poor; but they are often friends of the performers and appreciative, and they do prefer the real thing, even if it is a bit rough, to any recorded performance.'

Pru: 'The professional soloist would often be difficult to replace by an amateur, however outstanding. A top-class singer can lift a whole performance, will not break down in emergencies, requires less rehearsal time (and last rehearsals are always anxious) and can give the (possibly inexperienced) conductor much more confidence. My local choral society always brings in expensive soloists for these reasons, quite apart from the box-office effect.'

BWR: 'Looking back on your career as a whole, have you any general comments?'

Peter: 'I came into music as an amateur, and, if I had to choose between the amateur and the professional approach, I would certainly choose the amateur. There are, of course, many different kinds of professional; and, myself, I was very lucky to have in a way the best of both worlds, by starting straightaway in the Boyd Neel Orchestra (originally for 5/- per rehearsal) and continuing there for 15 years. Then came the War and the Merchant Navy – I managed to keep up the cello a bit (do you remember how I was once sent a skeleton "practising" cello by post, by our mutual friend Phyllis Woodward, and she forgot to include the F-holes?). After that, I managed to avoid the wearisome orchestra or theatre round, and found myself for many years with the Philharmonia, with the best orchestra and the world's finest conductors. Nowadays, I suppose I would go and play anywhere if sufficiently well paid, fed, and housed; but I would prefer a good amateur occasion without fee, if I could be sure of meeting some of my friends and of joining the high standard of musical understanding which I have often met in amateur circles. Perhaps I would like just one more top experience of the kind I have mentioned, a first-class performance with some worthy successor to Klemperer for choice.'

Pru: 'I agree with a lot of what Peter has said. For me there is nothing worse than playing with a group of professionals who have little interest in anything except the money – and only rarely anything better than playing with a group of committed amateurs. I will go anywhere to play music which I expect to enjoy.'

The singers have been rather poorly represented so far in this chapter; so it is good to be able to conclude it with the excited and exciting voice of *Paul Jennings*.

He was an (unconscious) collaborator with me in John Amis' B.B.C. programme, in 1975, 'Music Now', which was about amateur music. I gave a short talk about Music Camp, Colin Davis described the Chelsea Opera Group, Christopher Seaman the National Youth Orchestra; so we were in good company. Paul Jennings was speaking as a member of the New Philharmonia Chorus, and with his permission I give a precis of some of what he said (which I have on tape) – he put across a marvellous impression of the excitement and exaltation of singing a great choral work with a fine chorus.

'Think of 6.30 on Thursday evening in the middle of London –
everyone hurrying to get home – but you can see a few going against
the stream; they collect as a cheerful crowd in a warm room – then
the chorus master raises his baton, and what a marvellous sound it
all is. To me it's a symbol, an analogy, to heaven: the nearest you can
get to it. It's a splendid team we have – we've sung all the great
works, Verdi "Requiem", "Choral Symphony", Missa solemnis:
with Klemperer, Giulini, Boulez – you can't get higher than that.
Recently we sang the Missa solemnis four times in France – guests of
the French Government, and most hospitably treated. The further
we were from London, the more remarkable it seemed that this could
happen, 180 of us there together, making this glorious sound – but
then it is the English thing, the thing we do better than anyone else in
the world.

   And small groups of singers have the same devotion – there is one
just started near where I live in Manningtree, and there is just the
same feeling. Five or six of us used to travel by the same train from
Liverpool Street, and occasionally we managed to sing a madrigal on
the way, the number of parts being determined by the loss of our
bass, who got out at Chelmsford. I wanted to be a pianist, and no
man ever wooed a woman with more passionate devotion than I did
the piano; but hard work wasn't enough, and I was a dead loss. But
not so as a singer – and what more could I want than this?'

10
Coda: Why Music?

As a final chapter in this book, I should like to revert to a question already raised – why do we all do music in these ways? I have asked many friends questions of this kind – how did you come into music, what does it mean to you? and the preceding chapter 9 is largely derived from their replies. But few can give coherent answers to such enquiries, and if here I try to give my own answers I shall probably do little better.

To some of my friends, music was just one interest out of many possible ones, which gradually become dominant; others heard something quite casually which gripped them and made them determined to know more; some joined the local choral or orchestral society from motives not mainly musical to start with; some grew up in a musical family, and music was almost taken for granted as a preoccupation or a way of life. One of the best quartet violinists I have ever played with said just, 'I could not imagine myself doing anything else.' There are several (among whom I would count myself), not necessarily original musicians or composers, who recognise a continuous presence of something rather incoherent at the back of their minds, which comes to the forefront as some sort of music if they ever stop and think about it.

At many points in this book it must have been obvious that music means excitement and happiness to a great variety of people. If we confine ourselves to just one descriptive word for their emotions, perhaps we should choose 'fun'. It is fun to try to play a note in tune; fun to experiment at the console of a big organ, or of a modern synthesizer; fun to come in confidently with the other basses in 'Et iterum venturus est' in the B minor Mass; fun even to sit down to an evening of envelope addressing, if the result is to be an exciting musical occasion. I played once for Sir Hugh Allen, in an orchestra largely from Music Camp, accompanying the Bach Cantata Club chorus in the B minor Mass. As he opened the score at rehearsal, he said to me, 'now this is probably the last time I shall ever conduct the B minor Mass. I am going to *enjoy* myself.'

But 'joy', 'fun', 'happiness', are perhaps not big enough words to hold everything that we may feel in music. In a circular letter, prosaically concerned with some problems of organization, I said recently, '. . . the broad purpose of an (amateur musical) organization is presumably to give pleasure.' This remark was queried by a sensitive musician who read it: she said that, to her, music was essentially a thing of the spirit, ultimately a contact with the Divine; 'pleasure' was an inadequate word, however justified it might be in the immediate context.

On my desk there were recently two solid volumes – scores of Beethoven's 'Fidelio' and of Verdi's 'Falstaff', two of the greatest works in music. I had in prospect the great privilege of conducting an Act from each of these at a birthday celebration in a few months' time. I already knew them well; but I had to know them much better before I could worthily meet orchestra and singers on such an occasion. Just to handle one of these scores I found to be intriguing and exciting; it set up queries, anxieties, reproaches – have I fixed that second clarinet yet, and where is a harp player to be found? Who is going to sing 'Nanetta'? What is going to happen to our party if it rains really hard, and 200 people have to tramp round in the mud, or there is a power cut? These are all organizational rather than musical problems; but they are all part of amateur music, as I know it and love it. But if I open the score, and forget the unwritten letters and the demands of the telephone, then I shall begin to be absorbed in something quite different, the music itself. I shall become excited; I shall be hearing and imagining some of the passages which I have to help the orchestra to play; I shall hear anew the balance of a particular chord, I shall be swept along by the music; and I know that I may reasonably expect that at many places in rehearsal and performance the music will well up and take charge of me; that I shall be tremendously excited, oblivious (in one sense) of my surroundings; I shall be for a moment or two a prisoner who sees again the light of day, I shall be a young lover clasping his Nanetta in his arms, I shall even be the old rascal Falstaff, starting off the great fugue and inviting everyone to supper. This is music; this is why I want to do it.

These special feelings of what I must call spiritual excitement are not produced to order; they are not a matter of technique or of learned knowledge; they have perhaps an infectious quality, for they are more likely to occur in some corporate effort in music than to some solitary individual, at the piano or reading his score; the whole being sometimes greater than the part. Presumably the great ones of music know them more frequently than you or I; we all know the accounts of Handel writing the 'Hallelujah' chorus, and to read Berlioz' 'Memoirs' is to get a vivid impression of the exaltations and depressions of a creative genius at work. But the modest amateur may also experience them; here is Samuel Pepys, after hearing the wind music from Massinger and Decker's 'Virgin Martyr' – 'It is so sweet that it ravished me, and indeed did in a word wrap up my soul so that it made me really sick, just as I had formerly been when in love with my wife; so that neither then, nor all the evening going home and at home was I able to think of anything but remained all night transported, so as I could not believe that ever any music hath that real command over the soul of man as this did upon me.' (It is pleasing to note that down-to-earth Pepys in his next sentence says, 'and makes me resolve to practice wind music and to make my wife do the same' – what better advice could there be for the amateur?)

I expect that Pepys got over his 'sickness' quite quickly, and went on to enjoy his music the next day as most of us do – without self-analysis, and in a large variety of ways. We cannot expect to find any criterion of merit or value which can be applied equally well to the semi-delirium of a rock festival, the feelings of a quartet rehearsing a late Beethoven work, of a jolly chorus singing 'And He shall purify', or of an enraptured child hearing a violin for the first time and wishing to play it himself. But all such feelings may have, on occasion, some special ecstasy which is a main justification for music at its best, and perhaps might be proffered in part defence of mankind as a whole, in common with religious experience, a beautiful mathematical theorem, and first love, as against its torture chambers and mass starvation.

I am reminded of that excellent piece of science fiction 'The Black Cloud' by Professor Hoyle. When humans have established communication with the mysterious Cloud, which is re-fuelling itself at our Sun, and is itself a superior civilization to our own, the Cloud asks in effect how we can justify our existence on the Cloud's scale of values. Eventually a late Beethoven piano sonata is offered as evidence of something significant that our civilization has produced, and it is accepted by the Cloud as worthwhile.

I have a photograph from a magazine – I do not know its exact origin – which seems to me to reproduce as a picture, better than anything else I know, the essential spirit of Music which eludes precise description. It shows a cell or dungeon, mostly dark, lit only by a high-up barred window. In the obscurity the back of a seated 'cellist, hunched over his instrument, is to be discerned through the shadows. The light just touches the bald spot on the top of his head. It must be Casals, in an extreme of concentration; probably his bow is not even touching the string; he is alone with his music, and nothing else can matter to him.

The fun of music is easy to come by, and should be there at every rehearsal and meeting; the exaltation I have been trying to describe is not to be had on demand, but nevertheless it is, in the last resort, that which holds us together in chorus, orchestra or ensemble, and which makes worthwhile the labours of practice and the tedious chores of organization. Unless it happens to us often enough – perhaps in some favourite passage, under some inspired conductor, or associated with deep emotions of other kinds – we shall not indefinitely pursue the craft of music as amateurs.

Everyone will have their own favourite places in music, more likely than others to produce that gut feeling, that huskiness in the voice, that shiver down the spine. With me, for example, it could be the first few bars of the 'Missa solemnis' or chorale no. 73 in the 'St Matthew', 'Surely this was the Son of God'. Or in the last movement of the 'Eroica', at the Andante, where the clarinet weaves up and down round the tune in the oboe and violins. A long time ago I was conducting this passage at rehearsal one summer afternoon, and I looked across the orchestra in the dusty sunlit barn where we were playing, to see Edric Cundell standing listening at the back. He caught my eye, and laid his hand on his heart; it was clear that my favourite passage was also his, and that in that moment we were as one, two musicians together in music.

As the final sentence in this book, we can do no better than to say it with Shober and Schubert:

du hol - de Kunst, ich dan - ke dir da - für, du hol-de Kunst, ich dan - ke dir!

Appendices

The main part of this book has described much music, as a prime source of happiness and friendship.

But there are other ways of looking at music. As a professional scientist myself, I have naturally been interested in the kind of question about music which a physicist or a psychologist might wish to ask. What is good ensemble or good intonation, if it can be precisely measured? What are the limits of the human ear, in discrimination, frequency range, analysis, and so forth? These are important and fascinating questions, as long as the scientist realizes that the questions which are really important to the musician – is this a good performance, is this music great or trivial – are forever beyond his range. Musical Acoustics is a vast subject in itself, and this little book is certainly not going to set itself out as a textbook, even of the most elementary sort. (References to excellent books are given in the Bibliography.) In this Appendix I will only say a little about one aspect of modern science and technology which has interested me – its effect on the improvement (or the reverse?) of musical instruments; this, also with Appendix 2, will lead on to the physicist's approach to the intriguing question – what is a good violin? A third Appendix will describe some of the attempts, made for practical reasons, to put amateur performers on some relative scale of merit; then there will be a short summary of the balance-sheets of a few of the societies already described; and finally a Bibliography for the amateur musician. (This is perhaps a good place to mention a somewhat embarrassing likeness of name, which has occasionally brought me undeserved credit. When I was working at the National Physical Laboratory, Dr D. W. Robinson was Head of the Acoustics Section. Particularly over the telephone, I was sometimes regarded as the author of fundamental work on the sensitivity of the human ear, and on industrial noise measurement, in which subjects my colleague had an international reputation.)

APPENDIX I
Improvements in Instruments

In one sense, the instruments of Wagner's day have not been improved in the present century. We still pay a large price for a 1900 Steinway, we give recitals on an organ 200 years old, or copy as best we can a violin made 300 years ago. In another sense, everything has been improved in detail, by the labours of generations of skilled craftsmen and by improved manufacturing methods. But the scientist as such has contributed no new principles in sound generation or control; lip on reed, bow on string, or the beautiful escapement action of the piano, still serve to display the ultimate artistry of the performer.

The scientist has not been idle however. He nowadays understands much better how some instruments work, and can to some extent guide future developments in intonation and ease of speaking. Full definition and analysis of the qualities of good string tone still eludes him, but the prospect of specifying reliable methods for making good stringed instruments is at hand.

It is when the skills of modern electronics are applied to musical instruments that a revolution has happened, and is still happening: first the electric guitar, then the electronic keyboard in every conceivable guise, stimulated by the vast audience and commercial finance available especially for popular music today. Electronic instruments have only marginally affected the kind of music I have been concerned in myself, so that apart from the Brindley bassoon and the small electronic organ with which I am familiar, my knowledge is at second-hand. But it does seem to me that much of the serious as well as the popular future of music, for composer, performer and listener alike, must lie in this general direction.

Wind Instruments

The elementary textbook picture of these instruments – cylindrical or conical tubes, different partial tones excited by lips or reeds,

140 An Amateur in Music

effective lengths varied by slides, valves, or holes – is much oversim-
plified. The reality is complicated; the precise position and shape of
bell and mouthpiece has been arrived at by laborious experiment
and 'feel'; even now, instruments apparently identical in material
and dimensions are not identical in the player's hands. Though it is
no doubt possible to play in tune on an old flute or bassoon, it is
unquestionably more difficult than on a new one. The purists may
claim that they sometimes prefer the old instruments for their tone
quality; the modern instruments are surely more flexible, with a
bigger range of notes and dynamics, and more suited to the ever-
increasing technical demands made by the composer. The 'French'
horn, in England at any rate, has almost universally become the
'German' horn, i.e. the wider-bore instrument, with its more complicated valve system is preferred, because the certainty of attack
and intonation, even for the first-class professional player, is
superior. I remember a long time ago my friend Eric Halfpenny, a
noted expert in the older instruments, urging me to have the
'Quoniam' from the B minor Mass played at a performance on the
original (valveless) horn. I asked for a demonstration. Interesting
and agile as was the result, the uncertainty of a proportion of the
notes destroyed one's pleasure in listening; I am not saying that
no-one today could play this difficult piece on the original instrument, but merely that at that time none of the players available to me
could do so.

Simple theory says that given sufficient rigidity in the walls, the
performance of a wind instrument would not depend on the material
of which it is made. (I am not here of course referring to other vital
qualities, such as ease of manufacture, stability under hard wear and
changing humidity and temperature, etc.) I know many players who
have strong preferences for the quality of sound from 'wood' as
opposed to 'silver' flutes (or the other way round!); and distinguished players have had instruments built of gold and other expensive materials. (There is a composition by Varese called 'Density
21.5', the figure being the density of the platinum of the flute on
which the work was performed.) I am unaware of any experiments
on comparative tone quality of flutes except those of Coltman in
which three experimental flutes, one of wood, one of thin silver, and
one of heavy copper, were played with the same mouthpiece in
conditions where neither player nor audience knew which one was
being used. No difference could be detected, either by player or by
audience. The truth is, no doubt, as in so many experiments of this
kind, that in fact there is no difference: but in normal circumstances

the player will play better, and will therefore convince the audience that the instrument is superior, when after thousands of hours of practice he has formed a personal relationship with a particular instrument; or alternatively, or additionally, he has paid a lot of money for it and it has become part of his popular 'image' as a performer. It is also very difficult, and probably expensive, to carry out trials on the merits of instruments (I shall have more to say about this later, in regard to violins) in conditions when the answer is not prejudged by player or audience. It is also unlikely that anyone will manufacture an instrument with equal care and perfection when the material is unfamiliar, and the resulting market value is less.

As with flutes, there is evidence with brass instruments that only the thickness, i.e. the rigidity of the walls, is of importance to the quality of the sound produced.

Woodwind players are at the mercy of their 'reeds'; oboists in particular carry little boxes and knives with them, and fill in odd moments by a gentle scrape here and there, which may convert a bad reed to a good one – or the reverse. I have never seen an attempt to specify, in physical terms (shape, thickness, elasticity, etc.) the qualities of a good woodwind reed; they are elusive, since (in my own experience on the clarinet) there is no method of telling a good reed from a bad one except to try it on the instrument. One feels, as a scientist, that it should be possible to specify and then to construct a good reed; but I believe that such attempts as have been made have not been very successful, and the truth is probably that the market is so small that the research and development costs to make a really good article would be excessive.

There is only one basic redesign I know of a wind instrument in which modern electronics have been used – the 'logical bassoon' devised and constructed by Giles Brindley – himself a distinguished physiologist by profession.

Of all the woodwind, the bassoon is the one where expedients in design are most necessary. It is long – a speaking length of some seven feet on the lowest notes – and has to be folded back on itself to bring the finger holes within reach of the player; even then, complicated keywork is required at various points on the normal instrument. Several notes tend to be out of tune without special correction, some trills are very difficult, and the tone quality may be uneven over the compass. Perhaps the overcoming of these difficulties produces some of the fondness with which players usually regard their instrument, as is evident in the writings of Archie Camden.

The essential difference in the Brindley instrument is that the holes are covered not by fingers and normal keywork but by electrically-operated pads; and the fingers in effect operate switches which, through an electronic network, select the best combination of pads for the production of a given note. The finger keys can therefore be placed wherever is most convenient for the player, and the holes can be placed at the best position, acoustically speaking. The electrical network which joins them uses 'logical' units similar to those used in modern calculators and computers (hence the name 'logical'); and, for any key depressed by the player, chooses the best way of getting the note required. An electrical network is of course much simpler to design and easier to construct than any equivalent mechanical linkage. The fingering, from the player's point of view, becomes simple; there are no difficult trills or cross-fingerings, the notes speak more easily, and the tone is more uniformly graded over the instrument. There are many other unusual features, as might be expected when a highly original mind is applied to a new set of problems. One is that the whole instrument is kept at a constant temperature electrically, and variation of this temperature is used as a convenient method of tuning.

I first heard this instrument demonstrated by Giles Brindley one evening at Music Camp; having explained the general principles of design, he proceeded to play a few passages to show it off, including the famous solo entry at the beginning of 'Le Sacre du Printemps', which I imagine Giles would have regarded as beyond his capacity on a normal instrument. Subsequently he built a double bassoon on the same principles: this turned out to be a very satisfactory instrument and is in regular use.

I understand that when Giles presented himself with his bassoon for an Associated Board examination, there was some consternation among the judges at his request for access to an electric power point; it being argued that an instrument which needed a power supply could not be a bassoon. This of course raises a very interesting point, akin to the difficulties of permitting elaborate calculators in mathematics and engineering examinations; the person who can spend more money on his calculator may have an advantage over others. I wonder what would have been the reaction in Haydn's orchestra at Esterhazy if a new recruit turned up with a modern double horn or a set of pedal timpani!

In the percussion department, though most instruments (as far as I am aware) do not display modern technology in particular, the use of plastic heads for timpani is now widespread, and leads to more consistent tuning and a truer note (this may have some connection also with the usually flatter shape of the bowl (see chapter 9 of Benade's book [ref. 9]). I do not think that design has altered much in the other tuned percussion instruments (glockenspiel, xylophone, bells, etc.) though, of course, these instruments are much more in demand in modern orchestrations, and there is more incentive for amateurs to own and to play them well; such works as 'Chichester Psalms' and 'Belshazzar's Feast' can nowadays be put on entirely with amateur players, which would have been difficult before the War.

Keyboard Instruments

Even before the days of electronics, keyboard improvements were suggested. One such, at least, was commercially available for a short time. In the years 1882–84 a Hungarian nobleman, Paul von Janko, designed a keyboard in which all keys were of equal width, and arranged, black and white, a semitone apart, i.e. one rank was C, D, E, F sharp, G Sharp, A sharp; and the other was C sharp, D sharp, F, G, A, B. The total width per octave could now be smaller, so that the normal band could easily stretch more than an octave; and of course there were now only two possible fingerings for any scale, arpeggio, or chord in any key, and transposition became very easy. A small Vienna firm put pianos with this keyboard on the market, and there was considerable interest in the U.S.A. – Decker Bros. in New York made and sold Janko pianos, and a centre of instruction in their use was established.

In spite of their obvious advantages, and of display recitals and even some original compositions specifically for them, interest never became permanent enough for commercial success. A pity; perhaps such an innovation could have paved the way for corresponding reforms in notation, e.g. the 'Klavar' notation, which still survives to some extent.

Even if now it is possible to amplify and modify sounds almost without limit by electrical means, the designer of a keyboard instrument may still choose the well-established mechanism of stretched strings struck by hammers to produce the original notes. As long ago as 1935, when valve amplification was well known, but not transistors, I came across the NeoBechstein piano. This looked much like a normal Bechstein, but it had only a vestigial soundboard: a series of pick-ups (similar in principle to those used today on electric guitars and the like) gave signals to an amplifier and speaker system. The degree of amplification and the rate of dying-away of the notes could be controlled by the player, and to my ears the sound was very beautiful – slightly more harp-like in tone than that of a normal piano, but with all the piano's control in flexibility and dynamics, sounding excellent both in Bach and in Chopin. John Hunt used to give professional recitals on this instrument, and made some records. But it was probably a little before its time, and I believe disappeared in the War.

In the current decade, electric 'grand pianos' are made by more than one firm, which attempt to equal or surpass the sounds of a good concert grand, while improving on them in certain respects – cost and weight for example. I have had a little experience of the Kawai instrument. The keyboard and action is stated to be the same as is fitted on this firm's normal pianos. The strings are shorter so that the overall length is much less; there are two strings to a note, rather than three, for most of the compass. The pedal action and damping is normal. The weight is only about a quarter of that of a big grand, and the whole is designed for easy transport – the pedal unit detaches easily, the body tilts backward on a horizontal axis, so that the whole instrument can be lifted or pushed easily on its own castors, e.g. through a doorway or down steps.

Without amplification, the sound is that of a very small piano, useful perhaps for practice in a small room. With the amplifier switched on, the sound is most impressive, suggesting immediately the possibilities of a large hall and a Rachmaninoff piano concerto! One great advantage should be that with the modern design of frame, tuning pins, etc. it should be easy to tune and should hold its tune well even when moved around frequently.

Smaller, cheaper and less ambitious keyboards nowadays multiply in every music shop; various rhythmic backgrounds, and storage of the tunes you have just picked out, are to hand. Most of these instruments generate the notes by purely electronic means, i.e. there is no vibrating string or reed from which the sound is derived. This is a tremendous commercial market (in 'Science Abstracts' for 1983, there were over 400 entries describing new electronic circuitry for such instruments). The 'serious' musician may smile at the more flamboyant of these keyboards, some with their multi-coloured stop ranks, and a tutor telling you how to play and compose in three easy lessons. But he must come to respect the electronic organs, which when made by firms of the quality of Copeman Hart or Allen will stand comparison as musical instruments with the conventional pipe organ of the smaller kind. Such organs will be smaller and cheaper; they will be flexible in specification, easy to install, and will need much less tuning and maintenance. If, for example, a small church needs a new organ, I feel that the authorities responsible for finding the money should go and listen to some good modern example, and, if convinced, attempt to overcome the probable prejudice of their organist!

For many years we have had at Music Camp a small Copeman Hart organ, very similar in design to that used by Paul Steinitz for his concerts, which has served us excellently. It is a single four-octave manual, no pedals, but with a 'melodic bass' arrangement which can add 16ft tone to the lowest notes of a chord: it has 4 ft and 2 ft stops, a quint, mixtures, and a distinctive Gemshorn. It has been carried round the countryside in the back seat of an ordinary car, to many a concert, being ideal, e.g. as continuo in the Monteverdi 'Vespers' or the Bach 'Passions'; and has proved itself very reliable if handled with reasonable care.

Formidable new keyboards have however appeared in the last few years, the Rolls-Royces of the electronic musical world – the Synthesizers. It has been possible for a long time to build up a great variety of sounds and put them together into a sequence, perhaps either for a sound-effects programme or film accompaniment, or on its own merits as a serious musical composition. But this has in general been very laborious and has required expensive equipment. Now an instrument such as the Yamaha DB7 is on the market, costing some £1,500, no more than some enthusiasts spend on their hi-fi equipment; and with this, in effect almost any sound that can be conceived can be produced, under the control of a touch-sensitive keyboard. It is of course fascinating to play around with new sound effects; but considered just as a musical instrument, it is the most versatile one you can imagine. If I were anything of a keyboard player, with such an instrument, I should try to establish myself at the back of some good amateur orchestra at rehearsal, prepared to deputize for harp, celesta, glockenspiel, harpsichord, organ, bells, tuba, gong, etc. at will, as needed: all with very convincing effect.

Stringed Instruments

Is it likely that we can improve the violin? (In this Appendix, 'Violin' stands for 'any of the normal string family'.) The instruments that we play on for choice today are very little different from those of 200 years ago – some would say that they are not altered in any significant way. They will usually have longer fingerboards, a little more inclined to the body; they are strung more tightly, with heavier and stronger strings (the modern string is of course a major technical advance, as we might remember when we find ourselves paying several pounds for so inconsiderable an object). But granted that there has been little major alteration, the scientist is entitled to put to the musician the somewhat cynical question, 'Tell me, what violins are the best, and why?' To some people, this is not a question at all; they know the answer already. The best violin is a Stradivari (or something like that), with some secret attached to which Science has not found the answer – the age, the varnish, the 'ring' of the parent tree when felled down its native slopes, and so on. Even in better informed circles, it would be a brave man who dared to say that the new violin under his arm was the equal of the best from Cremona, in the company, say, of Messrs Heifetz, Alfred Hill and Menuhin. The performance of such gentlemen at the highest artistic levels suggests that their skill in listening, their ear plus their experienced brain, is likely to be superior to our own; and we cannot pass lightly over their probably unanimous opinions; even while we note that they can hardly be unprejudiced. From their earliest years they have been told that certain violins are much better than others, and this idea must have become an intrinsic part of the success, financial and artistic, of their distinguished careers.

Nevertheless, it is permissible to have at the back of one's mind the feeling that, if there is such a difference between the Cremona and the modern product as is indicated by reputation and price, it should be possible to show this difference in some way. Are these valuable instruments worth their cost to the player (neglecting of course the historical or antique value)? Are they more efficient, in some way or other, for the production of beautiful music, which is their primary purpose? In many other spheres, superior performance is measureable; we can for example compare a Rolls-Royce with a Mini, in reliability, quietness, speed, comfort, etc. by objective measurements on which everyone would agree (quite apart from the 'snob' value); and would have little difficulty in saying which we preferred in given circumstances.

To judge fiddles, either as player or listener, is a very difficult matter. Any of us who plays string instruments is in the habit of taking one up, playing it for a minute or two, and saying 'that sounds good', or 'a weak D string', or 'rather harsh on top'. We discount, if indeed we think about it, the heavy curtains of the room we are playing in, the humidity, the unfamiliar type of string or shape and height of bridge, and many other factors which can be important. Such judgements are necessary and have their value; but if we are honest with ourselves, we will remember that often we know what we want to think, and that the human ear is very subject to suggestion and is apt to prefer what it is used to; just as many people will prefer their old muffled loudspeaker system to any up-to-date hi-fi clarity. Also memory for such a thing as quality of sound is very short, and if one is choosing between two rather similar sounds, only a rapid and often repeated change from one to the other, if possible in random order, seems to me to have any validity in forming a judgement. (Personally, I find it hard to credit those people who maintain that, say, Madame A's top A in a particular aria, heard thirty years ago, was superior to Miss B's similar note, presently available to us.)

If we are going to search intelligently for a 'best' violin, we must think closely about what we mean by 'best'. There are many possible definitions:

(1) The 'best' violins are those which are owned and played by the 'best' violinist (it is easier to agree on a 'best' violinist than on a 'best' violin).

(2) The 'best' violins are those which fetch the highest prices.

(3) The 'best' violins are those which would be picked out, from a large number, as good to play on, by first-class violinists who do not know their age or value.

(4) The 'best' violins are those which, when listened to anonymously by a musical audience, played by good players (but not of the first rank) are judged to give the 'best' sound. (Here again we are in a difficulty of definition: does 'best' here mean 'loudest', 'sweetest', 'most penetrating', 'most uniform over the range of the instrument', or what?)

(5) The 'best' violins are those which best meet some physical criterion which can be objectively measured, e.g. a specified harmonic content over various frequency ranges, maximum total

energy radiated, widest dynamic range over which a note will 'speak' easily, etc., etc.

To make such distinctions may seem a fruitless hair-splitting to some enthusiast who has looked forward from childhood to inheriting his aunt's violin, with a magic if dubious Cremona label inside; or to the soloist who has been told so often how well his Strad fills this large hall. But though my detailed choice of words may be queried or improved, I do feel that the variety of these definitions emphasizes the arbitrariness of what we often say and think. Definition (1) is in fact the usual assumption of the layman (particularly the novelist). (2) is the basis for the success of several distinguished firms of instrument dealers. (3) seems a reasonable definition, and probably overlaps (1) to some extent; but it is very seldom strictly applied in practice, without pre-judgement. (4) would also seem a rational definition, if the main function of a violin is to perform music to be listened to; but it is very difficult (and tedious, and expensive) to apply fairly, and will be regarded as waste of time by the expert who works by a mixture of (1), (2) and (3), and thinks that he knows the answer anyway. (5) has great scientific interest, but is pointless from the standpoint of the practical player unless it can be correlated or calibrated in some way from the results of the other definitions.

Granted this correlation, however, (5) might lead to a more rational approach to violin quality, and to the production of larger numbers of good and reasonably-priced violins in the future. It has stimulated in the past half-century a lot of skilled research, about which I will say something shortly. First however let me describe some experiments concerned with definition (4).

To one who has never tried it, it might seem a fairly simple matter to get together a few violins, one or two players, and an interested audience: tell the listeners to shut their eyes, listen and vote. The reality, if the results were to carry real conviction, would be very different. We should need a representative collection of violins, including some of the world's finest; an assortment of players, including one or two of top rank; a patient and cooperative musical audience, including a few of those who claim, 'I can recognize the tone of a Strad, even over the radio'; a week's leisure for all (for experiments would have to be repeated several times); a comfortable hotel, in an attractive holiday spot, to keep everyone happy; and finally a millionaire, to pay for it all.

Of course, such an experiment will never be done. But there have been more modest attempts to ask and answer some of the questions relevant to our definitions of a 'good' violin.

For example, Saunders had copies made of the Italian instruments of the Curtis string quartet; these were matched to the older instruments as closely as possible, and when measured in the laboratory were found to give acoustic spectra (i.e. analysis of the sound radiated over various frequencies) almost identical. At a series of eight public concerts, the programme was terminated by a movement played on both sets of instruments in turn, the audience not knowing which set came first. The final audience vote of prefer- ence was convincingly for those instruments which were played last. On this evidence, there was nothing to choose between the sound produced by the two sets. (I have been told, in regard to this experiment, that the players themselves thought that they could play so as to make either of the sets the more attractive to the audience, as they wished.) Many trials on new instruments have shown that listeners cannot distinguish them as such from old ones. I have myself carried out (but not published) a few trials which aim at being statistically more reliable than is usual in this sort of experiment. The results, in which several instruments of a wide range in value, several players, and musical audiences took part, were not in general very conclusive. Details and further comments were given in Appendix II.

The experiments which I made contained the assumption that the 'tone' of a violin is adequately revealed by playing long steady single notes (mainly in order to eliminate technical and intonation differences between players). Pickering regards this as a fallacious assumption. He says (in a private communication), 'Audience listening tests are quite useless in determining the quality of an instrument. In the first place, there are as many acceptable violin "tones" as there are acceptable speaking voices, and only the ugliest are inherently unacceptable. Even those, however, may be made attractive by great artistry in use – instruments or voices.

'What the listener hears is the player, and if he is a fine artist he can make almost any instrument sound well by exquisite control of vibrato, bow velocity and pressure, bowing point on the string, and so forth. Not least in importance is the musical example used. Only a trained observer can extract useful information from a scale, and actual music introduces another variable – personal preference.

'If the listener is perplexed or confused, the player rarely is. His judgement is based on the relative ease with which he can produce the musical effects desired. This includes physical comfort – neck shape, height of strings, chin rest, etc. – as well as response to the bow in all registers.'

I think myself that Dr Pickering's attitude to listening tests is commendably suspicious; but if what he says is literally correct, it would appear that the judgement of the quality of an instrument, regarded solely as a device for the production of a beautiful sound, is even more subjective (and probably more arbitrary) than we normally assume.

Listening tests for quality come within the province of the auditory psychologists. Let us consider Boomsliter and Creel, in a very interesting recent paper, on 'The Auditory Characteristics of Violin Tone'. They maintain that unevenness (which is characteristic of most physiological processes, including playing the violin) is an essential part of judgement of pitch or tone. Synthetic sounds, lacking such unevenness, sound dead and unnatural. In one experiment, different forms of the same tune were recorded on tape, the only difference being that slightly different tuning systems were used in determining the pitches of the notes. When listeners were asked to comment on the different versions, 'the response was almost invariably about differences in tone quality – "this one has a richer harmonic content" or "this one has a heavier tone quality" or "this one is brighter". Rarely does anyone comment on pitch differences.' They go on to say, 'when a skilled player produces something that we experience as extremely good tone quality from an instrument, part of what we experience as good tone quality comes from his choice of exactly the right note tunings for the particular note pattern.' It would be interesting to know whether the same conclusion would be reached if the test pieces had been arpeggios (as in our listening experiments) rather than 'tunes'.

Altogether this paper by Boomsliter and Creel is unusual and thought-provoking, and could well be read carefully by all serious violinists. Perhaps one moral might be drawn from what they say – alas, some of us suspected this already – that the best way to make a violin sound better is not to play around with the soundpost or fit new strings, but to persevere over the years with slow practice for intonation and bow control!

If we are to believe an advertisement currently (1983) displayed in the London Underground Railways all this is a waste of time, and we are foolish in imagining that there are problems in recognising tonal

differences between violins. A well-known firm of loudspeaker manufacturers says quite positively, 'If you cannot tell the difference
between an Amati and a Strad on your hi-fi set, then you are not
using one of our loudspeakers.'

Let us now turn to an area of interest where results are more
definite, related to our definition (5) of a 'good' violin – the attempt
to make such objective measurements on a violin as to identify the
merits of its tone quality and perhaps to repeat them at will in the
making of new instruments.

Much research in this field originated with Frederick Saunders,
who was Professor of Physics at Harvard University. He died a few
years ago; but his work has continued through the 'Catgut Acoustical Society' (C.A.S.), devoted to the science of stringed instruments,
which is now world-wide in its connections, and has a most able and
distinguished leader in the person of Carleen Hutchins, who is a
scientist as well as being a first-class instrument maker. Review
papers (ref. 25) will give an idea of the difficulties and of the considerable progress which has been made.

In seeking to analyse the sound by which a violin produces, the
instrument may be stimulated in all sorts of ways – by bowing by
hand or machine, by vibrating the bridge or belly electro-
mechanically, or by a controlled impact. The resulting sounds are
received by a microphone and analysed as regards intensity and
frequency. The result may give a sort of 'fingerprint' of the instrument, perhaps as a graph of the response to different frequencies over
the audible range. Though a given instrument will usually give
repeatable and individual results, it has proved very difficult to draw
general conclusions from such records, e.g. comparing a batch of
'good' violins with 'bad' ones, or 'old' with 'new'. Nevertheless,
several experimenters have put forward figures of merit (usually a
combination of the measured responses over different ranges of
frequency) which they think compare reasonably well with the
merits, as judged by groups of players and listeners.

In addition, the sensitive methods of observation and analysis
which are now available have been used to study in detail more
specific problems, such as the motion of bow, string, and body; the
effects of different wood, thickness, varnish; and the phenomenon of
the 'wolf-note'.

Much of the research, particularly that guided by Carleen Hutchins, has resulted in a sort of rationalization of the methods used
intuitively in the past by skilled makers to produce good instru-

ments; in particular, the 'tuning' of the bare plates (back and belly) of the instrument before final assembly. If these plates are lightly supported and then tapped, they vibrate, and a note with a definite musical pitch will usually be heard. The differences between these notes have traditionally been used in the final shaping and thicknessing of the plates. Using more modern methods of exciting and revealing these vibrations, Carleen Hutchings has been able to suggest relationships between them which in her experience have led to a good instrument when the final assembly is made, and many instrument makers are now following the techniques which she has suggested.

One result of the C.A.S. researches has been an ambitious project – the design and construction of a 'New Violin Family' of instruments, acoustically like violins, but covering the full range of musical frequencies. In the normal string orchestra, the viola, cello, and bass are clearly different from the violin in tone quality; and of course this fact has great musical value and is fully exploited by composers. It seemed however an attractive and interesting project to produce a family of instruments, both higher and lower than the usual violin, but with as far as possible similar acoustics. The project could be regarded partly as a test of theoretical understanding, and partly as an experiment in new sonorities.

Over a period of years, eight instruments were eventually designed and made, ranging from a 'sopranino', strung an octave higher than a normal violin, to a 'contrabass' with the same tuning as a double-bass. Design was not easy, and could not always follow the scaling principles which theory would indicate: for example, the smallest instrument could not have strings too short for normal fingers to play (actually the string length is about ⅔ that of the violin); and the contrabass on the ideal scaling would have been unmanageable in length and girth. Nevertheless, with certain compromises a set of instruments was built in the 60s, and by 1972 a second set had been constructed and sent to England, where I had the pleasure of housing it in my studio in London for a time, and of finding keen players who were prepared to take the trouble to become familiar with the instruments and to demonstrate their qualities in several concerts. Since then, funds have been found to set up a studentship for a professional player to look after and experiment with the instruments, responsibility for the housing of which was taken over by the Royal College of Music.

Detailed descriptions and criticisms of the instruments are to be found in the literature (ref. 25). It is wrong to regard them as intended substitutes for existing instruments, though three of them at least could be played straight away by competent players – the 'mezzo' as a rather larger and more powerful violin; the 'baritone' as a large cello with particularly good bottom strings; and the contrabass, with the same comment: heavy to move around and large to hold, but a magnificent sound. The 'alto' was also a fine-sounding instrument, but was too long for a normal player to hold under the neck (though there is one professional player in the U.S.A. who uses it this way). In our team it was played by a 'cellist, using a long spike, as a very small 'cello; it did not take her long to learn to play it well, and she liked it because she now had a chance to play the viola parts in chamber music, hitherto denied to her!

At the time when I was familiar with these instruments (1976) my personal reactions were as follows: as a string ensemble, a beautiful and intriguing sound, rather different from that of a normal string group, smooth and homogenous, especially remarkable for its clarity and for the richness of tone of the lower instruments. I did not feel that the very small violin had enough to contribute, to make up for the difficult of playing it; but I think that with a real specialist on the instrument there might have been a lovely 'sheen' over the whole ensemble effect. The obvious problem was that of music to play; little at that time had been composed specifically for the new family, and one cannot live by arrangements alone! Music originally written for the viol family was of course pleasant on these instruments, but their much bigger tone and dynamic range were not appropriate.

As individual instruments for an amateur to play – again, a purely personal reaction: I played the mezzo violin for some weeks in chamber music, and would happily have continued to do so had there been need or opportunity. I am not a 'cellist, but had I been, I think I would have tried to get a baritone for my own use – I took it to show to Martin Lovett, of the Amadeus Quartet, and after playing it for some time against his own instrument, he said that he thought it tonally speaking the best modern cello he had ever tried. I particularly liked the basses, as an erstwhile player of this instrument: the contrabass was too big to move around for the amateur, though I did not find it too fatiguing to play when in position. The small bass was my particular favourite, quick-speaking and with a fluent tone; I took it to an orchestra once or twice, but of course its limited downward compass made difficulties. Had it been possible for it to have five strings (I do not know whether this was structurally possible) it would have been the ideal amateur's bass, with the further advantage that in a light case it could just be carried by a tall person (such as myself) in one hand, like a cello.

These comments are no criticism of the main purpose of the New Violin Family, which was to demonstrate a new approach to violin design. In this, it seems to me that the Family has been brilliantly successful. Interest has been maintained, particularly in the U.S.A., where several other sets of instruments have been built, and various concerts and demonstrations have been given. There are plans for a workshop-study-type conference for performers and composers, centred on these instruments, in Stockholm in 1985.

APPENDIX II
Violin Listening Tests

INTRODUCTION

In planning tests there are many difficulties to be considered.

1. We assume a large room, of reasonably good acoustic (not an anechoic chamber nor the reverberant showroom favoured by violin dealers); and that the instruments will be played behind a light (non-absorbent) screen, everything being arranged so that the judging audience has as far as possible no clues as to which instrument or which player is concerned.

2. In subjective measurements of this kind, it is good practice for each judgement to be between two choices only, presented as close together as possible, e.g. in the form 'I prefer A to B' (or the reverse). 'I have no preference' is to be discouraged as an answer. The tests – of course, in randomized order – should be short, for audience fatigue occurs very quickly; and repeated more than once if possible (as a minimum, we should have B against A as well as A against B).

3. For tests on violins, much argument is possible about

   (a) the time each player should spend in getting used to each instrument before the test, and the degree to which the instruments should be alike (e.g. in type of string, curvature of bridge, chin and shoulder rest). Some players feel that they can do justice to the tone of an instrument after quite a short time with it; others say that they will need at least a week to do so.

   (b) What is to be played for test? – remembering that about ½ minute is the total allowable time per test, if there are 30–50 tests, and the audience is to maintain its powers of discrimination. Also, should it be a phrase or two, at player's choice, on each string (as in series A below) or a steady slow passage of no musical content, as in the remaining series? Here we used a slow major arpeggio over three octaves, up and down, one bow to a note, starting on A flat to avoid open strings, taking about 20 seconds in all. (But it should be noted that some writers and some players maintain that the real 'quality' of an instrument is not likely to be displayed in such an exercise; also that players will tend to favour an instrument that seems to them to be 'responsive' or that 'speaks easily', and which in general flatters their own idea of their playing.)

4. In some tests, a few consistency checks (e.g. A against A) were included.

In the tests described here, (1) was always satisfied; (2) also, except in series (A); as to (3), the instruments used were not altered or fitted out in any way, except to make sure that the shoulder-rests suited the players; who in general did not feel that they were hampered in doing the instruments justice.

Of the dozen or so players who helped in these tests, about half were excellent amateur players; the others, young professionals. The judging audiences were by normal standards highly musical, largely made up of orchestral players and singers.

Series A: (January 1952)

Five violins: two players: 83 audience. Player's choice of a passage on each string; instruments and strings chosen at random. Assessed on tone quality, 10 for best possible, 5 average, down to 0 for very bad.

Violin	String: G	D	A	E	Average	Merit Order
Stradivari	6.59	6.44	5.09	5.29	5.85	1
Sanctus Serafin	5.40	7.52	4.24	3.36	5.14	3
Ceruti	6.47	6.96	4.49	4.80	5.68	2
Thir	5.09	5.97	3.44	4.00	4.83	5
Bowler	5.51	4.87	4.85	4.64	4.97	4

Each figure is the average of some 160 judgements, on the arbitrary scale of 0–10. The Strad is the best all round; the Serafin does better on the lower strings. The Bowler, a cheap and new instrument, does surprisingly well against an instrument 500 times its commercial value.

Series B: (October 1972)

Four violas: two players; five audience. Two test passages (Cadenzas from Brahms Quintet and from Mozart Concertante). 56 tests in all (4 × 3 × 2 × 2, plus 8 dummies, for consistency check). Tests given in two periods of 20 minutes – audience showed fatigue.

	Number of First Choices
Viola	(240 judgements: max. possible 120)
Guadaguini	35
English (?Duke)	56
Bollinger	61
Foster (junior)	88

These figures show a clear preference for the Foster, with little to choose between the second and third. The audience showed good consistency, repeating their own judgements well, and suggesting that violas are easier to distinguish than violins.

Series C: (August 1975)

Four violins: three players: 30 audience: arpeggio as test piece.

	Violin	A	B	C	D	No. of Judgements
Most	Player X	23.7%	31.2	18.0	26.7	264
Consistent	Player Y	25.3	30.3	16.2	27.9	264
Judges	Player Z	25.7	29.0	20.6	24.8	264
	All Players	24.9	30.1	19.4	26.4	792
All	Player X	24.6	30.4	19.1	25.9	360
Judges	Player Y	25.9	30.2	17.2	26.8	360
	Player Z	26.3	28.1	21.7	24.0	360
	All Players	25.5	29.5	19.3	25.3	1080

The above figures are given as percentages of 'first choice' judgements (if the four instruments were in a clearly recognizable order of merit, on which everyone agreed, then the figures would be 50, 33.3, 16.6 and 0 in one order or another).

The first set of figures is got by disregarding the results from 8 of the audience, who were shown by consistency checks to be less consistent than the others.

The violins were:

(A) The Mezzo violin from the 'New Family' made circa 1970 (cf. previous Appendix).

(B) Reindl of Mittenwald (1940).

(C) Ceruti (not the one of Series A), c. 1775; owned by Player Z.

(D) Guadagnini (1783); owned by Player Y.

All these violins would be regarded as good ones by most players; but (A) was unusual in construction (thinner, rather longer than most); and (D) was much the most valuable. There seems little evidence that the owner of a violin can therefore make a better sound on it than anyone else, or that the sound of the new instruments is inferior to that of the old.

Series D: (July 1982)

Four violins, two players, 36 listeners: arpeggio test piece.

This was a very similar test to that of Series (C), and two of the violins were the same, though the players were different.

Calling the violins A, B, C, D, then the first preferences were:

198 preferences for A
195 preferences for B (This was Violin C in series C)
243 preferences for C (This was Violin B in series C)
204 preferences for D

A completely random choice would have given about 210 preferences for each; and as before, if there had been a quite obvious order of merit, agreed by all, the figures would be in the set 420, 280, 140 and 0.

Choosing only the 15 most consistent judges, we obtain:

81 preferences for A
84 preferences for B
109 preferences for C
86 preferences for D

to be compared with the theoretical 'random' of about 90.

It is considered by my statistically minded friends that these differences are not big enough to have statistical significance.

The violins were:

(A) Man Seng Chan 1982 (the 9th fiddle he has made, Panormo model)
(B) Ceruti (as in Series C)
(C) Reindl (as in Series C)
(D) Andrea Guarnerius (1650)

The two players owned violins (A) and (C).

It is clear that once again the new instruments have done very well against the old.

Series F: (September 1982)

Six violins: two players: 48 audience: arpeggio test piece, as before.

These results were analysed more thoroughly (by a statistician) than the previous series. If 'no difference' judgements were discarded, the rank order was found to be:

Violin (A) 212 (ranking order: smallest best!)
Violin (B) 285
Violin (C) 351
Violin (D) 365
Violin (E) 310
Violin (F) 451

It was considered that the superiority of (A) and the inferiority of (F) was statistically established by these figures; the ranking of the other four cannot be made so confidently. It is interesting that the owner of the Montagnana, who was one of the judges, did not put this instrument on top in her judgements.

The violins were:

(A) Montagnana
(B) Bergonzi (1734)
(C) Ceruti (the same as in Series D and E)
(D) Gofriller (Francisco)
(E) A new instrument, maker unknown
(F) A German instrument, probably 1900

The violin (F) was originally included to help the audience by giving them an obviously inferior instrument as a sort of reference point. Nevertheless, one person ranked it top, and another as sharing the second place.

These tests have been a source of much interest, and I feel that they contain a lot of information about fiddles and players in general which could be extracted by a sufficiently industrious and expert statistician. I am very conscious of the criticisms which can be made of tests of this kind; I feel however that they show, for an average musical audience and average good players, that the quality of sound produced is not obviously correlated with age or value, however much the players might have preferred one instrument to another.

APPENDIX III
How Good a Performer are You?

There is no doubt that certain problems in the organization of amateur music would be less if there were available a reliable yardstick or index of merit, when dealing with a stranger. An evening's pleasure for several people can be wrecked by the introduction of someone who is notably worse, or perhaps very much too good, for the rest, or perchance doesn't fit in personally – though the last is a very rare event in my experience, as amateur musicians as a class could hardly be nicer people. But the problem is akin to that of the marriage bureau; the questions that matter are usually too difficult to formulate or to answer with sufficient candour.

But some efforts have been made, with partial success, to get a preliminary idea of how competent (also how willing and pleasant!) a stranger may be, though there is no real substitute for trial and error – or of course (in a large group) for regular audition, combined with the opinion of a few other experienced singers or players. On their own, very few people are able to give a convincing and dispassionate reply to the question, 'How good a performer are you?'

The Amateur's Exchange, a register organized by the Rural Music Schools Association in 1982, lists names and addresses, and a self-addressed merit, under the categories:

A A Diploma or equivalent
B Advanced: grade VIII etc.
C Intermediate: Grade VI/VII
D Elementary: Grade IV/V
E Beginner; Up to grade IV

Several people in the list do not attach a grade to themselves; others give variations, such as 'Passable', 'Med-Good', 'Ex-pro', 'Lowish' and so forth.

Applicants for an annual chamber-music course at Keele University a few years ago were asked more specific questions: thus, under the general heading 'Sight-reading':

Are you rhythmically and technically shaky until you know the piece?
Are you able to get to the end at the right time by knowing what to leave out? Are you nearly note-perfect in standard classical literature?
Are you more or less impeccable in all but exceptionally hard modern works?

and then, under 'Technique', having read a part a few times can you:
Keep going, even if you have to miss bits out?
Play a standard 2nd part, leaving the harder parts to someone else?
Cope with a Mozart string quartet/wind serenade?
Make something of a Romantic fast movement?
Dash off a concerto movement with some mistakes?

and then, under 'Experience', are you:
An amateur orchestral player who would like to play some chamber music?
An amateur who plays chamber music strictly at home?
An amateur who plays chamber music in public sometimes?
A music student at college? Which year?
A professional teacher who wants more playing?
A concert-giving professional?
It seems to me that these questions are well chosen, and that honest answers to them, taken all together, would give a very good idea of a player's merit. Mr George Pratt, who formulated them, tells me that the scheme has worked well, but that it depends more on his skill in reading between the lines than on the actual answers!
A more elaborate scheme has been used for some years by the American Chamber Music Players, which I reproduce, somewhat shortened, below. The questions for string players were formulated by myself originally, and when applied (in my own mind) to those players whom I knew well enough, they seemed to give the right 'pecking order'. Additional works for pianists and for wind players, and similar questions for singers, were added later by the A.C.M.P.

'Score 2, 1, 0 for each question, answering as honestly and objectively as possible, and add the result:

1. For how many hours a week do you do regular technical practice on your instrument – not just playing over difficult passages, but seriously aiming at technical improvement over the years? (Over five hours, score 2; one to five hours, score 1; otherwise score 0)
2. For how many years have you had fairly continuous lessons on your instrument? (Over 10, score 2, over three, score 1, under three, score 0)
3. How many hours a week do you play your instrument, on the average? (Over 10, score 2; over three, score 1, under three, score 0)
4. How often you have played a prepared programme to an invited audience? (Often, score 2; occasionally, score 1; never, score 0)
5. How many different players have you played with in your life? (hundreds, score 2; dozens, score 1; only one or two, score 0).
6. How many of the following (or their equivalents) have you played three times or more; the 30 selected Haydn quartets, the 10 well-known Mozarts, Beethoven op. 18? (practically all, score 2; a good many, score 1; a few only, score 0)
7. The same question and scores for – Beethoven opp. 59, 74, 95; Brahms 3 4tets and 2 string quintets, 4tets by Debussy, Ravel, Dvořák, Sibelius, Franck, Verdi?
8. The same question and scoring for – late Beethoven, Bartók, Reger, Hindemith, Shostakovitch, etc.
9. Imagine that you are playing a little known work of the difficulty of those mentioned in (6), with fairly good players. Would you be immediately conscious of a musical mistake (wrong rhythm, false entry, wrong modulating note, etc.) made by another player? (Almost certainly, score 2; probably, score 1; probably not, score 0)
10. Same as question nine, taking works mentioned in question 7.
11. You are asked to sight read, with very good players, something of the difficulty of the works of question 6. Would you be seriously lost at any point? (Probably not, score 2; possibly; score 1; probably, score 0)
12. Same as question 11, taking works mentioned in question 7.

Over 20 points in total is very rare among amateurs.

16 and over is EXCELLENT (A)
12 and over is GOOD (B)
 8 and over is FAIR(C)
 Under 8 is 'ETC' (D)'

The corresponding A.C.M.P. questions for singers were:

'1. Have you sung regularly through at least one year in one of the following ensemble groups:
   A. A rehearsing madrigal group with two or fewer singers to a part – score 2
   B. A choir or chorus with three to six singers to a part – score 2
   C. A choir or chorus with more than 6 on a part – score 1
2. Have you sung and practiced:
   A. Schubert, Schumann, Mozart, Brahms, Fauré Lieder? Score 1
   B. Strauss, Debussy, Weber, or Wolf songs with piano? Score 1
3. Are you asked to sing solos in Oratorios, Masses or Cantatas? Often, score 2; occasionally, score 1, not at all, score 0
4. How many of the following works (or their equivalent) have you sung in a performing group: Morley, Byrd, Wilbye madrigals; Palestrina or Byrd Masses; rounds of Purcell or Mozart; Baroque cantatas (other than Bach) or oratorios; Gilbert & Sullivan operettas; Bach Cantatas (complete cantatas, not just selections).
   Practically all, score 4; a good many, score 3; about half, score 2, at least three separate works, score 1; fewer than three, score 0.
5. Same as question 4, for the following (or works of equivalent difficulty): Brahms or Beethoven long choral works; Brahms *a capella* works, Bach motets, Russian choral music, early Debussy and five-part Italian madrigals; opera choruses, including Berlioz.
6. Same as question 4, for the following or their equivalents; *a capella* works by Stravinsky, Berger, Ravel; Hindemith; Gesualdo.
7. Imagine that you are singing a little known work of the difficulty of those mentioned in question 4, with fairly good singers. Would you be immediately conscious of a musical mistake (wrong rhythm, false entry, wrong modulating note, etc.) made by another singer? Almost certainly, score 2; probably, score 1; probably not, score 0.
8. Same as question 7, taking works mentioned in question 5.
9. You are asked to sight read with very good singers (two or three or more on a part) something with which you are unfamiliar, of the difficulty of the works mentioned in question 4. Would you be seriously lost at any point?

Probably not, score 2; possibly, score 1, probably, score 0
10. Same as 9, but holding a part by yourself (score 3, 2, and 0)
11. Same as question 9, taking works mentioned in question 6 (score 2, 1, and 0)
12. Same as question 9, taking works mentioned in question 6 (score 3, 2 and 0).

A total of over 33 points is very rare among amateurs.

27 and over is EXCELLENT (A)
18 and over is GOOD (B)
 9 and over is FAIR (C)
Under 9 is 'ETC' (D)'

APPENDIX IV
Some Financial Summaries

This Appendix will hardly be of concern to those who have no direct responsibility to the organizing of music; but I think it might be of interest, and even of help, to some treasurers or secretaries of musical societies. The figures here are very rough – approximations, sometimes even guesses – but I think they are reliable enough to illustrate the wide differences in financial problems which occur. I am most grateful to those who have taken so much trouble to let me have these figures, and to agree to their use here.

Many are more out of date than I could wish – one reason being that I started to collect this material some years ago. But since these are only a few isolated examples, chosen if at all for their diversity, I did not think that it would be worth worrying the kind people who originally gave me the figures, merely to update them perhaps by a couple of years. Anyone who looks at them must of course not assume that things are necessarily the same in 1985 as they may have been, say in 1981.

I give first the annual turnover (total of expenditure) in the year, as a measure of the financial size of the Society; then, expressed as a percentage of this turnover, under

Income
Subscriptions from members
Tickets (sometimes including receipts from Programmes)
Programme sales (with receipts from advertising in programmes if known)
Rent of property, if any
Interest from deposits or investments
Subscriptions from benefactors or 'friends of the Society'
Grants from sponsors
Grants from N.F.M.S., Regional Arts bodies or local Councils
'Self-help' (special benefit concerts, sales of work, etc. to produce funds)

Expenditure
Professional fees (usually for orchestra)
Soloist, conductor, accompanist fees

Management fees (e.g. in sale of tickets)
Salaries, commissions
Hire of Halls for rehearsals and concerts
Music purchase or hire
Rent, insurance, subscriptions, (e.g. to N.F.M.S.)
Instrument hire (e.g. pianos)
Printing and advertising
Postage, telephone
Miscellaneous administration

Unless one is particularly interested in any one Society, much detail is pointless; and I have usually had to run several of these headings together when summarizing the figures. Because of various omissions and approximations, the percentages will not necessarily add up always to 100%.

EDINBURGH ROYAL CHORAL UNION   1981/82
Turnover £15,000

Income		*Expenditure*	
Subscriptions	18%	Fees	67%
Tickets	52%	Printing, advertising	13%
Grants	12%	Hire of Halls	9%
Interest	4%	Salaries, commission	4.5%
Music Hire	3%	Rent, Insurance	4%
Miscellaneous	3%	Music & Inst. hire	1%
Fund Raising	7%	Miscellaneous Admin.	1.5%

LONDON ORPHEUS CHOIR   1981   Turnover £15,000

Subscriptions	13.7%	Orchestras	32%
Tickets	58.2%	Artists, Commission	23.7%
Programme sales	6.4%	Conductor, Accompanist	14.4%
Donations	7.4%	Hire of Halls	11.1%
Fund Raising	7.2%	Music	1.8%
		Printing, advertising	16.1%
(Deficit	−5.3%)	Miscellaneous	1.4%

(I think there was no N.F.M.S. support, and the finances have altered a lot in the past couple of years, owing to different I.L.E.A. arrangements.)

CHELSEA OPERA GROUP   1981–1982   Turnover £11,500

Income		*Expenditure*	
Subscriptions	15%	Fees	51.5%
Ticket sales	63%	Hire of Halls	12.7%
Gifts, sponsors, and fees		Hire of Music	3.3%
for accompaniment	22%	Printing, Advertising	13.4%
		Miscellaneous Admin.	8.8%

(No N.F.M.S. support. This was a good year financially, owing to favourable accompanying engagements; the balance restored losses in the previous year. Very dependent on ticket receipts.)

MARY WAKEFIELD
WESTMORELAND FESTIVAL 1981   Turnover £12,680

Entry Fees	5.2%	Orchestras	37.3%
Ticket Sales	35.2%	Conductors, soloists	
Grant (Northern Arts)	29.8%	adjudicators	18%
Grant (Local Authority)	8.9%	Hire of Hall & Stage	17.1%
Local Sponsors	20.8%	Music, Perf. Rights	5.8%
		Miscellaneous, Admin.	10.5%
		Put to Reserve	11.2%

(A very different picture; high dependence on grants, with comparatively modest spending on professional help. I was told that the 1983 accounts were very similar.)

NEWCASTLE UPON TYNE BACH CHOIR SOCIETY
(1980–1981)   Turnover £3,190

Subscriptions	29.8%	Fees	51.5%
Tickets	34%	Printing	1.8%
Programmes	3.1%	Music provision	13%
Self-help	8.3%	Postage	0.5%
Grants	23.0%	Subscriptions	
Tax rebate & Interest	3.7%	(N.F.M.S.)	1.7%
		Administration	2.6%

(There is a considerable credit balance; and a freedom from many normal expenses, showing economy and no doubt assistance from the University facilities.)

W.11 CHILDREN'S OPERA
(average of 1983 budget and 1984 forecast)   Turnover £5,000

Income		*Expenditure*	
Performer's subscriptions	15%	Composer's fees	18.5%
Ticket sales	55.4%	Orchestra & Conductor	7%
		Instruments and Music	11.2%
		Production fees	9.4%
		Staging & Lighting	34%
		Miscellaneous Admin.	17%

(This emphasises the very different financial problems of a stage production, even in an amateur setting, and though much professional help is in fact given without payment. Presumably the big gap between in- and out-goings was covered by help from interested parents and friends; it does not appear on the balance sheet.)

WOKING CHORAL SOCIETY   (1979–1980)
Turnover £5,670

Subscriptions	30%	Fees	42%
Tickets & Programmes	48%	Hire of Halls	13%
Interest, etc.	6%	Music Hire	3%
Grants & Donations	10%	Printing & Advertising	15%
Self-help	6%	Administration	8%

(This gave a surplus of 5% for the year. I chose this year from the several balance sheets which were offered me, because the three concerts in this year were of about average expense; some later concerts were by special arrangement with the N.F.M.S., and involved unusually large expenses.)

EDINBURGH SYMPHONY ORCHESTRA
(1980–1981)   Turnover £1,690

Subscriptions	16%	Conductor, soloists	12%
Tickets & Programmes	50%	Hire of Halls	21%
Benefactors	11%	Hire of Music	11%
Miscellaneous	10%	Printing, advertising	15%
		Miscellaneous – piano hire, N.F.M.S. subscription, repairs, secretarial	31%

(This seems an admirable balance sheet for a small Society. Money is carefully spent in the right places, and there are no problems.)

WELLS CATHEDRAL ORATORIO SOCIETY
(1981–1982)   Turnover £6,000

Income		*Expenditure*	
Subscriptions	25%	Fees	80%
Tickets, Programmes	40%	Hire of Halls	8%
Donations, sponsors	6%	Music Hire, pianos	6%
Grants	15%	Printing, postage	4%
Self-help	10%	Publicity	2%

(The 82/83 estimates assume an increased turnover of £7,000 because of rising costs, and will be met by increased subscription and fund-raising).

EALING SYMPHONY ORCHESTRA   (1982)   Turnover £900

The information about this Orchestra is best put in a slightly different form.

It has an income of about £500 (excluding ticket receipts), in about equal shares from member's subscriptions, grants from N.F.M.S. and local bodies, and 'Friends of the Orchestra'. It runs three or four concerts each year, each of which makes a loss of up to £100; a typical budget might be:

Receipts		*Expenses*	
Sale of tickets	£130	Use of church (with	
Sale of programmes	£10	heating)	£40
Sale of refreshments	£10	Fees or honoraria	
		(conductor, soloist,	
		leader, etc.)	£150
		Hire of music	£20
		Publicity, programmes	£50

In total, then, the Orchestra is able to pay its way, including N.F.M.S. subscription, general publicity, and miscellaneous administration costs.

In conclusion, I give details about four other groups mentioned in this book, which have the great financial advantage that they do not deal with public audiences.

ACCRINGTON CLEF CLUB   (1981)   Turnover £510

Income		*Expenditure*	
Member's Subscriptions	89.5%	Refreshments and	
Deposit Interest	6.7%	Entertainment	57.5%
Miscellaneous profits	3.6%	Insurance	6.5%
		Piano tuning	2.7%
		Rent	13.2%
		Miscellaneous	6%

(These figures do not include a special item, major repairs to the piano, which over two years cost £965; this sum was almost completely met by special subscription within the Club.

This seems to me an ideal balance sheet for a small amateur society. Some 90 members pay £5 each, mostly spent on their own entertainment at meetings, with very modest overheads, and something in hand for emergencies.)

OXFORD & CAMBRIDGE MUSICAL CLUB
(1981)   Turnover £1,860

Subscriptions and		Programmes, printing,	
Donations	81%	postage	29%
Dividends and		Music Hire	12.5%
Interest	19%	Room Hire	14%
		Miscellaneous	6%

(A surplus for the year. The Treasurer points out, 'The expenses in 1981 were particularly low, and I expect them to rise sharply in future years, with a probable increase in subscription in 1983. The Club's present strong financial position is due to strict control of expenses, and the rule that it does not pay outside players except in extreme emergencies.')

EDINBURGH SOCIETY OF MUSICIANS
(1981–1982)   Turnover £4,100

Income		*Expenditure*	
Subscriptions	26.8%	Rates	67.5%
Hire of Rooms	31.2%	Heat, Light, 'phone	10.7%
Donations	13.7%	Repairs	2.4%
Interest	1.4%	Printing, Postage	8.1%
Miscellaneous	1.8%	Accountant, Tax	6.6%
		Miscellaneous	4.5%

(These figures showed that the ownership of a valuable property, far from assisting the Society, was in fact a crushing load owing to the heavy rates. Since then, the Society has successfully applied for charitable status, and has also sold some of its historic property; so that the future financial position has been much improved).

MUSIC CAMP   (1981–83 averaged)   Turnover £10,130

Music Camp is certainly the 'odd man out' in this company. Its income is (for the purpose of this analysis) entirely derived from member's subscription, which is £39 for a period of 9 days, during which time the main expense is in the provision of food (say 1,450 person-days for each period), accounting for 60% of the whole expenditure. There is also:

Building maintenance, electricity, heating, rates   13.2%
Supplies (mostly equipment repair and renewal)   8.3%
Administration (post, telephone, insurance,
    printing)   11%

The surplus, say 7%, covers music hire and purchase in the main.

Bibliography

What follows is no attempt at a complete bibliography for the amateur musician, such as a reference work or a scholarly essay might offer; it is just a mention of those publications which I have come across and which seem to me to be of possible interest to the amateur. References in the text correspond with numbers here.

Dictionaries

One feels that all musical dictionaries (in English anyway) must be founded on the noble work of Sir George Grove, himself an amateur in music of the highest distinction! The first edition of 'Grove' (4 vols, 1894) can still be interesting reading, the assessments of Brahms and Berlioz, for example (Elgar, though born in 1857, has no article). The Preface explicitly states that 'the Dictionary is designed for the use of Professional Musicians and Amateurs alike.'

The practical handbook for us all is surely Scholes' masterpiece 'The Oxford Companion to Music' (1938, many subsequent editions, the last in 1983). This still remains what it called itself, a 'Companion'; it contains pretty well all the information that most of us want, a short plot of an opera, facts about a particular composition, a summary of a composer's life. It is abundantly cross-referenced; you can open it anywhere and browse, following the references, for half an hour at any time with pleasure and profit. The fact that it is written in effect by one person and in one (sometimes pungent) style gives it compactness and ease of reference, and Scholes does not mind tackling general articles on subjects which would daunt most of us. Even the last edition, 'New Oxford Companion' ed. Arnold, in two volumes, revised and extended, preserves something of the personal quality of the original.

The 'Harvard Dictionary of Music' (2nd edition 1970) is a handy reference for certain things, and has much more musicological detail about early music than Scholes; it has good cross-indexing and references to literature. There are brief notices of some operas and individual compositions, but nothing about composers separately; it is unusual to find a Dictionary of Music which has no article about Beethoven or Bach!

Cobbett's 'Cyclopedic Survey of Chamber Music' (orig. 2 vols, 1929, new edn. with 3rd volume by Colin Mason 1963) is a very full account of chamber music at the time of its writing; Cobbett's own enthusiasm as an amateur performer is apparent, and there are interesting articles about the history and organization of amateur chamber music. The judgements of musical value do not agree very well with those of most players today, though still of interest; thus late Beethoven is regarded as too difficult for the amateur, and Bartók is hardly mentioned.

The Fifth Edition of Grove's 'Dictionary of Music and Musicians' (1954 in nine volumes, with a supplementary volume in 1961) was amazingly good value when it came out in paperback some years ago; the binding is not robust, but it has lasted well enough with me; and the whole is not too big for the domestic bookshelf. It contains all the detail about composers and their works, and about some performers, that I am ever likely to need; the general articles are good and comprehensive.

And now of course comes the 'New Grove' (1980), in twenty imposing volumes. Here surely is everything that can be usefully written down about composers and their works, many performers, musicologists, writers, etc. and a lot about musical instruments. It spreads its net over the whole world, rather than just the English-speaking parts of it, and gives much attention to jazz and popular music; to quote from the Preface, 'it seeks to discuss everything that can be reckoned to bear on music in history and on present-day musical life.' It seems, however, that to the editorial board, the amateur is not an important part of 'present-day musical life'. One feels almost that, to the writers of some of the articles, 'amateur' is regarded as a dirty word. By reading appropriate portions of selected articles, it is possible to deduce that the amateur exists; for example, the articles on 'Cambridge', 'Dresden', 'Chorus', 'Leeds', 'London', 'Liverpool', 'Education' and 'Vienna', taken together, would lead to such a conclusion. There is a big article on Brass Bands and information on Festivals. There is no mention that I can find of the Amateur Chamber Music Players – a large organization with 6,000 members and international standing. One or two amateurs appear by name – Pepys, Britton, Evelyn, Herschel, Cobbett, and the 'Russian Five', for example. But, Mr Sadie, might not a few thousand of your many millions of words have been devoted to a general survey of the importance of the amateur in music – a difficult article to write, I admit!

The 'New Grove' is hardly suitable for browsing – which is not of course its intended purpose. But a good index volume with cross-references, similar to that of the 13th edition of the 'Encyclopedia Britannica', would be a great help in finding out whether any particular topic was somewhere included.

Smaller Works of Reference

1. British Music Yearbook (Annual, publ. Rhinegold)
   Meant for the professional, but has a mass of information of interest to the amateur, with some general articles of interest, and demonstrates the size and variety of the music industry.
2. National Federation of Music Societies – Register of Members and Handbook
   (obtainable from N.F.M.S. (Francis St., London SW1). List of societies (concert societies, choruses, orchestras) with address of federal representative and of secretary, size of membership, etc.
3. Music: a Report on Musical Life in England. Published on behalf of the Arts Enquiry set up by the Dartington Hall Trustees (1949)
   A detailed and factual survey up to about 1945, with a considerable chapter on Amateur Music.
4. Music and the Amateur. A report prepared for the Standing Conference of County Music Committees, National Council for Social Service (1951)
   Fairly detailed report on history and organization, especially of the County music advisers, County Music Committees, and Carnegie money. The section on amateur orchestras is obviously written by one who knows!
5. Making Music. A journal which ran for about 30 years (till August 1976). Up to this point it was subsidized by the Rural Music Schools, and had a joint editorial board with the Standing Conference of County Music Committees, charged with publishing 'Making Music' as an organ to speak for amateur music as a whole.
6. Youth makes Music: Report by the Standing Conference of Music Committees (National Council for Social Service) (1957)

Pleasantly-written propaganda and advice on starting a group of young people to make music together, at any level of skill.

7. Directory of Music Centres in the United Kingdom (Publ. Amateur Music Association, 43 Renshaw St., Liverpool L1 2SF (1983)
Addresses and names of about 250 music group and centre organizers.

Books

8. Aulich & Heimeran, 'The Well-Tempered String Quartet' (trans. Millar Craig, Novello, 1938)
Has been a popular book among amateurs, light-hearted and containing good advice, but fashions have changed, and estimates, e.g. of the importance and difficulty of the works listed, are sometimes strange to a later generation.

9. Benade, A. H. 'Fundamentals of Musical Acoustics' (O.U.P., 1976)
First-class and up-to-date exposition for the musician who knows a little science, or the professional acoustician who is starting on the subject. Very good at elementary description and its development to more advanced ideas; good material on musical instruments and the way we listen.

10. Blom, Eric, 'A Musical Post-Bag' (Dent 1941)

11. Bowen, Catherine Drinker, 'Friends and Fiddlers' (Little, Brown & Co., U.S.A., 1935)
A very personal account of a clever and dedicated chamber-music family. Some might feel it over-sentimentalized; I do not feel it this way myself.

12. Camden, Archie 'Blow by Blow' (Thames Publishing, 1982)
Entertaining autobiography by a top-rank professional, an amateur at heart.

13. Coleman, H. 'The Amateur Choir Trainer' (O.U.P., 1932)
Advice on church choirs, simple voice training, sight reading, etc.

14. Coward, H. Choral Technique and Interpretation (Novello, 1914)
Detailed account of choral training, especially for large choirs; a classic in its field. Coward was the outstanding choir trainer of his generation.

15. Franklin, David 'Basso Cantante' (Duckworth, 1969)
Autobiography of a varied career; interesting contacts with amateur music.
16. Galway, James 'An Autobiography' (Chappell, 1978)
Interesting for its picture of an original and determined child, growing up in a poor background with music all round.
17. Gertler, Andreé 'Advice to Young Quartet Players' ('Score', no. 5, 1951, pp. 19–32).
Excellent article, meant for young professionals, but valuable for the experienced amateur.
18. Gollancz, Victor 'Journey towards Music' (Gollancz, 1964)
Family reminiscences of a very experienced and sensitive listener, especially about opera.
19. Griffiths, Paul 'The String Quartet' (Thames & Hudson, 1983)
Not about playing, nor a list of works, but a scholarly study of the development of the musical form of the quartet. Continues up to very modern composers, though it avoids comparisons of musical merit. Could suggest many ideas to those rehearsing thoughtfully.
20. Haigh, Gerald. 'The Schools Prom' ('Chorale', vol. 2, no. 3)
Comments on the influx of youthful singers into choir singing and its profound future importance in the development of music.
21. Halsey, Louis 'The Art of Choral Conducting' ('Chorale', vol. 2 1982)
A series of helpful articles; realistic comments on intelligibility, diction, etc.
22. Haweis, Rev. H. R. 'Music and Morals' (Strahan & Co., 1871) and 'My Musical Life' (Longman, Green, 1902)
Wide-ranging comment on many musical aspects of the period; expert on bells and violins, biographies of several musicians, and his own experiences; distinguished players; exposition of Wagner; the musical scene in general. Interesting to dip into; very popular books in their day.
23. Higham, David 'Literary Gent' (Jonathan Cape, 1978)
Witty and perceptive account of what music (among other things) meant to him as a devoted and experienced amateur singer.
24. Hurd, Michael 'Vincent Novello and Company' (Granada, 1981)
Interesting information about music, mainly choral singing, over several generations of the firm.

25. Hutchings, C. W. 'A History of Violin Research' (Journal of the Acoustical Society of America, 73(5) May 1983)
    Authoritative survey by the leading expert in this field, with about 200 references to previous work.
26. Ibberson, Mary 'For Joy That We Are Here' (Bedford Square Press, 1977)
    Delightful and moving account of the growth of the Rural Music School movement, 1929 to 1950, by its chief inspirer and leader.
27. Jennings, Paul 'Vox Pop' ('The Times', 10 Dec. 1983)
    The pleasures and excitements of choral singing in Great Britain.
28. Knight, Freda 'Cambridge Music' (Oleander Press, 1980)
    Personal account of music at Cambridge, mainly amateur and University, from 1500 onwards, with much interesting historical background.
29. Loesser, Arthur 'Men, Women, and Pianos' (Simon & Schuster, 1954)
    An unusual book. The development of the piano (and earlier keyboards) is used as a framework for much musical and social history, detailed and scholarly, often pungently and amusingly expressed. Solid reading, best in small doses, but not to be missed.
30. Mackerness, E. D. 'A Social History of English Music' (Routledge and Kegan Paul, 1964).
    The later chapters are a sensible and wide-ranging survey of changes in the musical scene in the present century (the only book in which I have found a reference to Shera's book, see below).
31. Norton, M. D. Herter 'The Art of String Quartets Playing' (Gollancz, 1963) Detailed study of examples for practice, discussion of dynamics, etc. and summary of references on this subject.
32. Page, A. 'Playing String Quartets (Longman, Green, 1964)
    An excellent book, equally for the advanced amateur as the professional student. Realistic and comprehensive remarks on all manner of subjects; comments on performance and repertoire, from Haydn to Bartók.
33. Patterson, Blake. 'Musical Dynamics' (Scientific American, November 1974)
    Good semi-popular article, with measurements of the performance of amateurs and professionals on a variety of instruments.

34. Paynter, J. and Aston, P. 'Sound and Silence' (C.U.P., 1970)
    Classroom projects in creative music.
35. Pierce, J. R. 'The Science of Musical Sounds' (Scientific American Books, W. H. Freeman, 1983)
    Unusual and exciting book, on which it is difficult to make adequate comment in a few works. From the familiar basics of sound and hearing, we are led simply yet with elegance to a fresh approach to musical perception and the possibilities of new (computer-designed) sounds.
36. Radford, Maisie and Evelyn. 'Musical Adventures in Cornwall' (David & Charles, 1965)
    Charming account of the work of the Radford sisters in promoting amateur music, especially opera, with small resources, in Cornwall, 1920 to 1960.
37. Rorke, J. R. M. 'A Musical Pilgrim's Progress', and 'The Latchkey to Music' (O.U.P., 1942)
    One person's attempt to explain how he feels about music
38. Seashore, C. E. 'Psychology of Music' (and other publications) (originally McGraw Hill, 1938; modern reprint in Dover Publications, 1967)
    The original classic research on what the musician really does (pitch, rhythm, vibrato, etc.) when measured in the laboratory.
39. Shera, F. H. 'The Amateur in Music' (O.U.P., 1939)
    Short but delightful survey of the history of amateur music, essentially in England. The final pages reinforce some of what is said in the present book, but of course were written before the changes of the past 40 years.
40. Spohr, Louis 'Autobiography' (translated from the German; Longman, Green, 1865)
    Interesting reading, for the different attitude of performers and audience to chamber music, 120 years ago.
41. Steinitz, Paul 'On Rehearsing a Choir for the Canticum Sacrum' ('The Score', no. 19, March 1957 pp. 56–59)
    Excellent advice on rehearsing a choir (small and good amateurs) in difficult and unfamiliar modern music.
42. Thorne, Graham 'The Oxford and Cambridge Musical Club' (private publication)
43. Young, Percy 'George Grove' (Macmillan, 1980)
    An excellent biography; what one 'amateur' can do in music!

Novelists

Though hardly relevant to the subject-matter of this book, perhaps I might be allowed to remark that novelists as a whole either avoid any revealing description of music, or are ill-informed and unhappy about it. Lord Peter Wimsey is unconvincing when he sits at the piano to play Bach; and there are occasionally real 'howlers', as when a distinguished detective novelist, an excellent writer, makes her villain, a clarinettist, play with the gramophone through the *slow movement* of Bach's Third Brandenburg Concerto. There are, however, honourable exceptions; thus Edmund Crispin knows what he is talking about in a Bach Choir rehearsal, and Cyril Hare makes the basic plot of one of his stories depend on the orchestration (i.e. no clarinets) of a Mozart symphony. He also gives so convincing an account of the efforts to obtain a replacement professional player at the last moment from the neighbouring city, that I feel sure he has acted himself as the secretary for an amateur orchestral society!